Enjoy!
Mona

To Dad With Love

by

Mona Meittunen Abel

To Dad With Love

Published by
MagnumFX, Inc.
P.O. Box 337
Side Lake, MN 55781

Illustrations, book, and cover design by
Steve D. Mayer of MagnumFX, Inc.

Web Design by Lee M. Carlson of MagnumFX, Inc.

Web Hosting by www.MagnumFX.com

Printed By Sentinel Printing, St. Cloud, MN 56304

http://www.cookbooksbymona.com
email:mona@cookbooksbymona.com
ISBN 0-9769455-0-9

THIS COOKBOOK IS LOVINGLY DEDICATED TO NOT ONLY MY DAD AND GRANDFATHER, BUT TO ALL MEN FROM MINNESOTA'S IRON RANGE.

At a book signing in Hibbing, after my first cookbook was printed, our wonderful, retired school nurse Jennie Salo came in and bought many books from me and said, "Now you have to do one for your dad". It never occurred to me that I would be doing another book but; I have had the time of my life. Of course, my friends tell me that I could have the time of my life in a phone booth.

The stories have been the fun part. The Iron Range is full of wonderful characters and so many stories to tell. I wish I had space for more.

Special thanks to my new friend Steve Mayer who just recently started his own business with Lee Carlson, Magnumfx.com. Steve is an enthusiastic and optimistic person with great skills and admits he is a computer nerd. He has worked very hard on this cookbook and has helped the stress level tremendously. Maybe not for him, but for me.

Thanks to all that sent me recipes, stories and pictures. A special thanks to my wonderful friend Margy Retica Hughes who proofread all the recipes and made me change the word "prick" to "poke" (as in a cake that you prick holes and add sauce).

Check out my website cookbooksbymona.com as I will be doing a monthly newsletter and will need your input.

Thanks for buying my cookbook!

Mona Meittunen Abel
"Recipe Diva/Former Go Go Dancer"   May, 2005

Cover Picture: My Cornish Grandfather William Jack Williams and Finnish Dad John Eric Meittunen at the new well on the Iron Junction Road 1942.

INDEX

INDEX

INDEX

INDEX

Stories cont....

My Dad

**1935 Graduate of
Chisholm High School**

John Miettunen

**"School is place to
study and learn.
Only in Vacation to
pleasure may we turn."**

Appetizers &
Beverages

Mario Retica about 1955
story on page 150

BEET PICKLES
Bill Ruskanen's favorite

1 c. water
1 c. vinegar
1 c. sugar
½ tsp. cinnamon
½ tsp. cloves
½ tsp. allspice
Lemon slices, use about two slices per jar
About 4 cups of beets, scrubbed

Boil beets until the skins will slip off easily. Simmer above ingredients until sugar is dissolved. Thinly slice the beets and simmer for 15 minutes. Put in very clean jar, cover with above ingredients and refrigerate.

Tip: to clean hands from getting purple from beets, cover hands with vegetable oil.

HERBED SHRIMP DIP
1 lb. shrimp, cooked
2 green onions, coarsely chopped
1 shallot chopped, or use garlic
2 T. chopped fresh tarragon
1 c. mayonnaise
1 c. sour cream
½ tsp. Worcestershire sauce
½ tsp. hot pepper sauce or more

Put shrimp, green onions, shallot and tarragon in food processor. Using on-off turns, process until shrimp is finely chopped. Transfer to bowl, mix in mayonnaise and next three ingredients. Season to taste with salt and pepper. Cover and chill at least 2 hours. May be made a day ahead.

BOAT: A HOLE IN THE WATER SURROUNDED BY WOOD INTO WHICH ONE POURS MONEY.

CHUTNEY CHEESEBALL

2 oz. pkg. cream cheese
½ tsp. curry powder
1-10 oz. jar chutney, drained
½ tsp. dry mustard
Sliced almonds

Mix all ingredients and roll in sliced almonds.

GREAT CREAM CHEESE DIP

11 oz. cream cheese
1 can Rotel tomatoes with green chilies (do not drain)
1 pound cooked and drained Jimmy Dean sausage

Mix together – that's it!

SMOKED SALMON ROLLS

1 pkg. smoked salmon
4 oz. garlic and herb cream cheese
1 T. minced fresh dill and 1 tsp. dried dill weed
8 oz. refrigerator crescent rolls
2 T. capers, drained (optional)

Heat oven to 375 degrees.

Flake salmon and combine with cream cheese and dill in a bowl.

Pat out crescent roll dough on a lightly floured surface into a 14x9" rectangle. Pinch perforations closed.

Spread salmon mixture over pastry; sprinkle with capers.

Roll pastry lengthwise; pinch seam to seal. Cut into ½" thick slices; place slices on a lightly greased baking sheet.

Bake for 12 minutes. Serve warm.

Makes 10 to 12 appetizers.

OVEN CARAMEL POPCORN

Our family friend Amy Gustafson's recipe is the best! I thought I had lost it and it didn't get in the first book. I would eat so much of this at Christmas, I would be sick to my stomach.

6-7 qt. popcorn
Nuts optional

2 c. brown sugar
1 c. butter
½ c. white corn syrup
1 tsp. salt
Boil above syrup for 5 minutes
Remove from heat and add 1 tsp. baking soda and 1 tsp. butter flavoring.

Stir well over popcorn and spread on cookie sheets (2 – 9 x 13 pans) and bake at 200 degrees for one hour. Stir every 10-15 minutes. Cool and eat.

ORANGE HONEY NUT POPCORN

2 qt. popped corn
1 c. mixed salted nuts or almonds
½ c. butter or margarine
½ c. honey
1 T. grated orange rind
¼ tsp. cinnamon
¼ tsp. nutmeg

Melt butter; add rest of ingredients. Boil gently for one minute. Stir constantly. Drizzle over popped corn and nuts. Bake at 350 degrees for 15 to 20 minutes. Stir every 5 minutes.

PICKLED FISH
From the garage of Thomas Tylla

Makes one gallon
Hint: 1-1/2 to 3 pound northerns or suckers make the best pickled fish.

Clean and cut up the fish into slabs that will fit into a wide mouth gallon jar and will lay flat when you place them in the jar. Roll the slabs of fish in a cake pan of canning salt. A cup of salt is enough for a one gallon recipe. Put slabs of fish in the jar on top of each other. Place a weight (example: a smaller covered jar filled with water) on top of the fish. This will keep the fish from floating in the water that will be created during the curing process.

Fill the gallon jar half full with slabs. This can be done over a period of time if you can't catch enough fish in a day. All the fish in the gallon jar must cure for a minimum of one week. Fish can be left in the jar indefinitely. Note: the fish get firmer the longer they are in the salt.

When the time is right for you (1 week to whenever), pour contents of the gallon jar into a colander. Rinse each slab with water once. Cut the rinsed slabs into bite sized pieces. Rinse the gallon jar and put the pieces back into the jar. Fill the jar with enough white vinegar to cover the pieces. Let the pieces soak in the vinegar for 24 hours. Then pour the fish and vinegar into the colander discarding the vinegar. Do not use this vinegar again.

Boil the following for five minutes:
2-1/2 c. sugar	1 tsp. whole allspice
6 c. white vinegar	3 tsp. white mustard seeds
4 bay leaves	1-1/2 tsp. pepper corns
1 tsp. whole cloves	7 red chili or chile peppers

Let cool to room temperature. Add 2 cups of port wine, (or use your discretion as to amount – this may be too much for some people) 2 medium sliced onions (opened apart into onion rings), and 1 sliced lemon. Put a colander on another pot and pour the brine ingredients into the colander to separate the solids from the liquids. Hand mix the solids with the fish as you loosely pack them in the gallon jar. Try to pack a large portion of the solids (lemons, onions, peppers, bay leaves, seeds and corns) next to the glass so you can see them. This gives the jar a nice look. Pour the liquid portion of the ingredients into the jar, filling the jar to the top or close to it. Let stand in the refrigerator for three days to one week to allow the ingredients to blend. Important: fish is to be refrigerated at all times during the making of this recipe. Note: smaller jars could be used after running them in dishwasher.

TOMATO SANDWICH

4 slices whole wheat bread
4 slices white bread
1 onion, grated
1 c. mayonnaise
Black pepper
2 tomatoes, sliced
Seasoned salt
1 bunch parsley, optional
1 bunch basil, optional

Begin by cutting the bread into circles with a biscuit cutter or cookie cutter. Combine the grated onion, mayonnaise, and black pepper. Spread mixture onto the cut out bread circles. Cover and refrigerate.

To prepare the tomatoes, peel, slice, and drain thoroughly between layers of paper towels. Sprinkle the tomatoes with seasoning salt before assembling the sandwiches. Place a tomato slice on top of the whole wheat bread. Top with parsley or basil. Place the white bread on top of each stack. Prepare the sandwiches several hours before the party. Cover with a damp towel and refrigerate until ready to serve.

FRUIT DIP

2-8 oz. cream cheese, softened
1 c. powdered sugar
2 T. orange juice
½ tsp. vanilla

Blend well. Serve with fruit. Refrigerate.

Tom's son Len Tylla told me this Finnish joke: Toivo said to Eino, "my 50th wedding anniversary is coming up and I don't know what to do for Olga". Eino said, "what did you do for her on your 25th"? Toivo said, "I took her to Finland". Eino said, "that was great". "Yes," stated Toivo, "maybe I'll go and pick her up".

ASPARAGUS CANAPES

1 T. mayonnaise
1-15 oz. can asparagus
1 loaf thin sliced bread
Melted butter
4 oz. Roquefort cheese at room temp.
(it calls for 8 oz. – depends upon your taste)
8 oz. cream cheese at room temperature
1 egg, beaten

Cut crust from bread. Roll bread flat and spread with mixture made of both cheeses, mayonnaise and egg combined. Roll one stalk of asparagus in each bread slice. Secure with pick. Dip each bread roll in melted butter. Place in freezer for a short time. Cut each roll into thirds. Bake at 350 degrees for 15 minutes. Note: These can be made ahead and frozen until you want to serve.

CUCUMBER SANDWICHES

These are so good and so British!

1 pkg. whipped cream cheese
1 pkg. Good Seasons Italian salad dressing mix
Cucumber, sliced thin
1 pkg. pumpernickel bread or party sandwich size

Combine cream cheese and salad dressing mix. Spread small amount of mixture on each slice of bread. Slice cucumber and place one slice on each cream cheese slice.

Chevrolet announced 1934 prices:
5 window coupe - $565;
sport coupe with rumble seat - $605.

CHOKECHERRY WINE

A recipe sent to me from Lucille Method that she received from Norbert Arnold originally from Pengilly, MN. See story in back of book.

1 gallon chokecherry pulp (ground coarse)
10 c. sugar
1 gallon water, lukewarm
1 pkg. dry yeast

Place this mixture in a crock, cover with a newspaper and a cloth and place in a room temperature place. Stir morning and night for at least two weeks. After this time, sample for sweetness. Strain and fill into bottles or jugs. Wine will ferment additionally after bottling. DO NOT close tightly for at least three weeks after bottling. Can then be put in a cool place.

Do not use a blender for grinding cherries (I wrecked mine doing so). We've used a meat grinder clamped to an old chair with newspaper to catch drips as you work.

CHAMPAGNE ON YOUR PONTOON

Makes 18 cups of punch

1 pkg. sugar-free ruby red grapefruit mix and 8 cups of cold water
1 tsp. sugar-free orange drink mix
2 bottles of extra-dry champagne
1 liter club soda

Mix all ingredients and head straight for McCarthy Beach!

"Old is when......A sexy babe catches your eye and your pacemaker opens the garage door."
"Old is when......An all nighter means not getting up to pee."

CHRISTMAS GLOGG (mulled wine)

Cousin Bob Miettunen from Sarasota, Florida sent me this recipe. He and his wife served this at affairs during the Christmas season and it also is a tradition at his sister Hazel Holmquist's home. In both Finnish and Swedish the umlauted "o" is pronounced as "er". The most similar sound in English would be the "ur" sound in "curtain".

1 bottle of red wine, burgundy or cabernet sauvignon (jug wine is okay)
1 small packet of spices tied in a cheesecloth square 4 to 5". Place in it – 1 tsp. whole cloves and ½ tsp. of grated fresh nutmeg
3 or 4 sticks of cinnamon
1 or 2 cups of vodka
Raisins, almonds

Pour wine into a stainless steel saucepan; add bag of spices, cinnamon sticks and ¼ c. of raisins and 15 to 20 almonds.

Heat and bring to simmer, do not boil as that will dissipate the alcohol in the wine.

Remove from heat and add vodka and again bring it to a simmer (do not boil).

Remove from heat, remove spices. Pour into glass serving cups. Make sure there are some raisins and almonds at the bottom of each cup.

Serves 6 to 8 persons.

A man was telling his neighbor, "I just bought a new hearing aid and it cost me $4,000, but it's state of the art." "Really", answered the neighbor. "What kind is it?" "Twelve thirty."

FINNISH RHUBARB WINE
From Gene and Sister (Walters) Wilenius

3 quarts rhubarb, cut fine
3 lbs. white sugar
1 pkg. (about 2 tsp.) dry yeast
1 gallon cold water

Do not use metal containers. Use glass, plastic, or crocks well washed. This makes one gallon. If you multiply it, don't increase the yeast. Put rhubarb in large container (5 gallon plastic pail works good). Add the cold water, stir and cover tightly. Let this stand for ten days and if there is any mold, just skim it off. After ten days, skim off all the fruit and strain through cheesecloth. Add sugar and yeast. Cover and let stand four days stirring once daily. Bottle and loosely cork for 60 days. Add a heaping teaspoon sugar to each bottle to make a sparkling wine.

Seal and stand in cool place. This improves with age.

MOJITOS
Cuban drink that Kenneth Mackey from Ciao Restaurant in Side Lake made for us – mmm!!

Make simple syrup consisting of 2 cups of sugar and 2 cups of water. Stir over medium low heat until sugar dissolves. Add 1-1/2 c. fresh lime juice and 16 mint leaves (crush or macerate mint leaves to release flavor).

Add 2 cups of lemon rum and add club soda and ice to taste.

MOJITOS (a simpler version)
3 sprigs mint (macerated)   3 T. lemon or lime juice
2 tsp. sugar   1½ oz. light rum
Club soda

Macerate mint sprigs, add sugar and lemon juice in a tumbler. Add ice, rum and club soda.

A husband is someone who, after taking out the trash, gives the impression that he just cleaned the whole house.

PEACH MARGARITA

Makes 2 cocktails. Use the ripest, juiciest peaches you can find and slice them over the blender so you don't waste a drop of nectar. Use unsweetened frozen peaches if the fresh fruit is out of season. Be careful – these fruit cocktails are so delicious that you tend to forget they contain alcohol.

2$\frac{1}{4}$ oz. tequila
2 oz. triple sec
3 oz. freshly squeezed lemon juice
4 oz. simple syrup*
2 peeled, pitted and sliced fresh peaches
                or
1$\frac{1}{2}$ cups partially frozen peach slices
4 c. cracked ice

Place all the ingredients in a blender until smooth. Pour the mixture into a margarita glass.

*To make simple syrup: Heat equal parts sugar and water to the boiling point. When the sugar has dissolved, remove from the heat and let cool. Keep in a capped bottle (does not need refrigeration).

LETHAL WEAPON

Use your imagination for amounts of each..

Absolut Vodka
Peach Schnapps
Cranberry Juice
Dash of lime juice on top

I'm so depressed. My doctor refused to write me a prescription for Viagra. He said it would be like putting a new flagpole on a condemned building.

CALIFORNIA WHITE WINE COOLER
Great at the deer shack!

2 oranges
2 peaches
12 strawberries
½ c. sugar
Lime slices
4/5 qt. chablis

Peel oranges and cut into segments. Peel and dice or slice peaches. Wash and hull strawberries, cut in half. Combine fruits in pitcher and sprinkle with sugar. Add wine, splash of champagne or soda, serve in stemmed goblets.

HONEY AND CIDER VINEGAR DRINK
Remedy for "What Ails You"

2 tsp. honey
2 tsp. vinegar
Mix together and put 4 tsp. in glass of water. Drink before bed.

SWEDISH GLOGG
This recipe is symbolic with Swedish hospitality and Christmas festivities.

1 bottle domestic brandy Few blanched almonds
1 glass red wine
3 sticks cinnamon
1 c. sugar
10 whole cloves
1/3 c. seedless raisins
6 cardamom seeds

Heat the spices in sufficient wine to cover them and cook gently for 15 minutes. Make the Glogg a few days in advance. Bottle and seal tightly. Serve the beverage hot with a few raisins, almonds and bits of fruit peel.

Beverages

RHUBARB COLLINS
Now you know what to do with that abundance of rhubarb!

4 lb. rhubarb stalks, trimmed and cut into ½" pieces
2 c. sugar
6 c. water
¾ to 1 c. fresh lime juice
1 (750-ml) bottle gin (optional)
1/3 c. Cointreau or other clear orange liqueur
2 (1-liter) bottles seltzer water, chilled
16 small lime wedges

Bring rhubarb, sugar, and water to a boil in a 5 to 6 quart heavy pot, stirring until sugar is dissolved, then reduce heat and simmer, partially covered, until rhubarb falls apart, about 15 minutes. Remove from heat and cool 15 minutes.

Pour mixture into a large fine mesh sieve set over a large bowl and drain 15 minutes, then press gently on and discard solids. (There will be about 8 cups syrup.) Skim off any foam and cool syrup to room temperature. Pour syrup into 1 or 2 pitchers and chill, uncovered, until cold, about 2 hours.

Stir in lime juice (to taste), then gin and Cointreau. Fill glasses with ice and add rhubarb gin mixture, stopping about 1" from rim. Top off with seltzer. Run a wedge of lime around rim of each glass, then squeeze into drink.

Note: rhubarb syrup (without lime juice, gin, or Cointreau) can be made 1 day ahead and chilled, covered, or frozen 1 week.

"Relationships are hard. It's like a full time job, and we should treat it like one. If your boyfriend or girlfriend wants to leave you, they should give you two weeks' notice. There should be severance pay, and before they leave you, they should have to find you a temp."
Bob Ettinger

SMOOTHIE
From my nephew Evan Sundquist, the Track Decathalon Man

2 T. peanut butter
¼ c. oatmeal
1 banana
½ c. milk
¼ c. plain or vanilla yogurt
1 T. honey
2c. ice cubes

Blend in blender until smooth. Makes about 24 oz.

BERRY SMOOTHIE
From my nephew Reid Sundquist, the Ironworker

1 c. berries (whatever you have on hand)
½ c. milk
1 T. honey
Dash of vanilla
½ c. yogurt
2 c. ice cubes

Blend in blender until smooth.

GIN AND RAISINS
An old English recipe

12 oz pkg white raisins
3/4 c. white gin
Boiling water

Pour boiling water over raisins and drain. pour gin over raisins. Let set for one week. These keep indefinitely.

(An old english remedy for arthritis was to eat 12 of theses gin-soaked raisins every day. Even if it didn't help your arthritis, you were a very happy person.)

Cakes/Cookies/Bars/Candy

John Borovac story page 164

BANANA FLIPS

1 yellow cake mix
1 pkg. (3 oz.) banana instant pudding
4 eggs
1½ c. milk

Mix ingredients for two minutes on low. Pour evenly into two jellyroll pans that have been lined with wax paper. Bake 350 degrees for 14 minutes. Let cool.

Prepare filling:
1 c. butter
½ c. milk
1 c. sugar
3 T. flour
1 T. banana extract

Beat five minutes. Spread over one cake. Flip other cake on top. Cut and wrap into individual servings. Freezes well.

GERMAN BUNDT CAKE

This recipe came from a German friend in Minneapolis – Margaret Hagar who moved back to Germany many years ago.

Grease pan generously (Crisco) and make design with almonds and cherries.

Mix together: ½ c. sugar
           1 T. cinnamon
Sprinkle 1/3 of this mixture over almonds and cherries.
Pour 1 c. buttermilk over 2 oz. of poppy seed – soak for 15 minutes
Cream together: 1c. butter and 1½ c. sugar
Sift 6 times: 2½ c. flour
           1 tsp. baking soda
           ½ tsp. salt
           2 tsp. baking powder
Separate 4 eggs

Add beaten egg yolks to cream mixture. Add 1 tsp. of vanilla or almond extract. Add flour and buttermilk with poppy seed alternately to cream mixture. Beat egg whites stiff and fold in. Pour ½ the mixture in pan, then sprinkle with the rest of the sugar and cinnamon mixture. Add remaining batter. Pour into Bundt cake pan (or use a spring form pan or angel food cake pan). Bake 1 hour or more (10 minutes) at 350 degrees. May be served with whipped cream.

ORANGE CAKE

Dick Marinucci's grandfather's recipe from the turn of the century when he worked in a monastery in Italy. Dick (we always called him Tilly) wrote a cookbook called "Treasures of the North Woods".
A story from Tilly's book about Aho's Pool Hall can be found in the back of the book.

¾ c. fat (Crisco)
1-1/2 c. sugar
2 eggs
3 c. flour
2 tsp. soda
2 c. sour cream
Juice and rind of 1 orange (grated)
1 c. chopped raisins

Bake in a 9 x 13" pan at 350 degrees for 40-50 minutes. Frost with thick powdered sugar frosting and nuts. To make the frosting more flavorful, use orange juice instead of milk and put grated orange peel in the frosting.

MANDARIN ORANGE CAKE

2 c. flour
2 tsp. soda
2 tsp. vanilla
2 eggs
2 c. sugar
1 tsp. salt
2 c. drained Mandarin oranges
For cake: Combine all ingredients in mixer bowl and beat with mixer until well blended. Pour into a greased 9 x 13 pan. Bake at 350 degrees for 35 minutes.

For frosting:
1-1/2 c. brown sugar
6 T. milk
6 T. butter

Combine ingredients in a saucepan and bring to a boil. Boil 3 minutes. Poke holes in the hot cake and pour hot frosting over it slowly.

POPPY SEED CAKE

3 c. flour
½ tsp. baking powder
3 eggs
1-1/2 c. milk
1-1/2 tsp. almond flavoring
1-1/2 tsp. vanilla flavoring
½ tsp. salt
2-1/4 c. sugar
1-1/2 c. oil
1-1/2 T. poppy seeds
1-1/2 tsp. butter flavoring

Mix together and bake in greased and floured bundt pan 1 hour at 350 degrees.

FRUIT CAKE

Dick Noble sent me this great recipe

4 oz. fruit bits
4 oz. dried raisins
1 railroad tie
Wood saw
Large rubber mallet
Safety goggles

Cut a one-foot section from the middle of your railroad tie. The resulting block of wood should be the size and shape of a loaf of bread.

Take the fruit bits and raisins (five-year old raisins are preferred) and pound them into the block with your rubber mallet. Spread the colors around, or you might wind up with an ugly fruitcake. Don't be afraid to throw some elbow grease into that mallet! Good fruit bits and dried raisins should be much harder than the railroad tie, so you can't break anything.

For best results, you should pre-treat the fruit bits by setting them on top of your garage for a year (or by microwaving them on HIGH for 30 minutes).

Finally, cover it tightly in plastic wrap and decorative paper with a lovely bow on top and give your loved ones the timeless and enduring gift of fruitcake!
WHOEVER EATS FRUITCAKE ANYWAY?

Bars/Cookies

Uncle Darrel Tonneslan, married to my Aunt Perky Williams
"What a hood'
(Taken during the Korean War)

YULE TRIXIE'S

A favorite company recipe at the Retica house especially after athletic events at 615 East 23rd Street.

Delectable brownies with a creamy peppermint filling.

1/3 c. shortening
½ tsp. vanilla
1 c. sugar
2 well beaten eggs
2 squares (1 oz.) unsweetened chocolate melted
2/3 c. enriched flour
¼ tsp. salt
1/3 c. chopped walnuts (optional)
¼ c. chopped raisins (optional)
1 T. cream or "top milk" (remember that?)

Thoroughly cream shortening, vanilla and sugar, add eggs. Beat well. Stir in chocolate, add sifted dry ingredients. Mix thoroughly, add nuts, raisins. Stir in cream. Spread in two 8" square pans (wax paper lined).

Bake at 350 degrees for 20 minutes. Cool.

Put layers together with Trixie Cream in middle – make sure you put the top layer on with top side showing.

Trixie Cream:
Combine 1T. hot milk, 1 tsp. butter, ¼ tsp. peppermint flavoring and 1 c. powdered sugar. Blend.

Spread on one of the 8" pans. Peel off wax paper.

Cut and store.

NEW COMPANY RULES – Restroom Use
Entirely too much time is being spent in the restroom. There is now a strict 3 minute time limit in the stalls. At the end of three minutes, an alarm will sound, the toilet paper roll will retract, the stall door will open and a picture will be taken. After your second offense, your picture will be posted on the company bulletin board under the "Chronic Offenders" category.

CHINESE CHEWS

½ c. butter
2 T. sugar
1 c. all-purpose flour

Cut butter into the flour and sugar as in pie crust and pat into bottom of a 8x8" square pan. Bake 15 minutes at 350 degrees.

2 eggs beaten lightly
1-1/2 c. brown sugar
1 c. coconut
½ c. walnuts

Spread over crust and bake 10 to 15 minutes longer.

PECAN PUFFS

1 c. butter
4 T. powdered sugar
2 c. pecans, ground
1 tsp. vanilla
2 c. flour

Cream butter, add sugar and remaining ingredients. Roll into small balls, bake in 325 degree oven for 30 minutes. Roll in powdered sugar when hot and again cold. Yield 2 dozen cookies.

"If life were fair, Elvis would be alive and all the impersonators would be dead." - Johnny Carson

CHOCOLATE MINT COOKIES

This recipe was Mary Retica's "stand-by". This was Sylvia Baraga's recipe, she was a great cook and wonderful person.

¾ c. butter
1½ c. brown sugar, packed
2 T. water
Heat above until butter is melted

Add 1-12 oz. package of chocolate chips. Stir until partially melted. Remove from heat and melt completely as you stir. Put all in large bowl and cool 10 minutes. At medium speed, add 2 eggs, reduce speed and add:
2½ c. flour, all purpose
1¼ tsp. baking soda
½ tsp. salt

Beat on low until blended and refrigerate for one hour. Roll into teaspoon size balls and bake at 350 degrees about 11 minutes. Remove and immediately place ½ of an Andes mint on each cookie and spread when melted. If you make teaspoon size, it will make about 9 dozen cookies. If you make a larger cookie, you will want to use a full mint.

POTATO CHIP COOKIES

This is what you do when you have stale potato chips.

1 c. shortening
1 c. white sugar
1 c. brown sugar
2 eggs
1 tsp. vanilla extract
2 c. all-purpose flour
1 tsp. baking soda
½ tsp. salt
2 c. crushed potato chips
½ c. chopped walnuts (optional)

Preheat oven to 350 degrees. In a large bowl, cream together the shortening, white sugar and brown sugar until light and fluffy. Add the eggs one at a time, beating well with each addition, then stir in the vanilla. In another bowl combine the flour, baking soda and salt.

continued...

32

Cookies

POTATO CHIP COOKIES continued...

Gradually stir into the creamed mixture and continue to mix until well incorporated. Finally, fold in the potato chips (and walnuts, if desired). Drop by rounded spoonfuls onto an ungreased cookie sheet. Bake for 8 to 10 minutes. Allow cookies to cool on baking sheet for 5 minutes before removing to a wire rack to cool completely. Makes 5 dozen medium-sized cookies.

Candies

CARAMEL PECAN TURTLES
Love any kind of turtles!

1 c. Crisco or 1 Crisco stick
1-1/2 c. sugar
½ c. brown sugar
2 T. milk
3 eggs
1 tsp. vanilla
4-5 c. flour
1-1/2 tsp. baking soda
1-1/2 tsp. cream of tartar
1 tsp. salt

Caramel and Chocolate topping:
28 caramels
2 T. milk
3 c. pecan halves
1-6 oz. bag semi-sweet chocolate chips

continued...

From the Bear River Journal...April 30, 1914
"Notices have been posted for the application of postmaster at Side Lake, and an office is likely to be established soon."
(From Gloria Anderson Hegg)

CARAMEL PECAN TURTLES continued...

Cream Crisco shortening and sugars together. Add milk, beat in eggs one at a time, add vanilla. Combine flour, baking soda, cream of tartar and salt. Mix into creamed mixture. Chill one hour. Heat oven to 350 degrees. Roll out 1/3 of dough at a time, to ¼" thickness on a floured surface. Cut out with 2¼" cookie cutters. Place 2" apart on ungreased baking sheet. Bake 5-6 minutes, until edges are slightly golden. Remove to cooling rack. For topping, combine caramels and milk in microwave-safe bowl. Cover with waxed paper. Microwave at 50% for one minute. Stir, repeat until smooth (or melt on range top in small saucepan on very low heat). Drop rounded teaspoonfuls on top of each cookie.

Place 3 pecan halves around edge of caramel. Place chocolate chips in microwave-safe cup, microwave at 50% for one minute. Stir. Repeat until smooth (or melt on range top in small saucepan on very low heat). Spread rounded teaspoonfuls over top of caramel.

Don't cover pecans, cool completely. Makes 5 dozen.

CHOCOLATE TRUFFLES
You have to try making these – they are awesome!

¼ c. heavy whipping cream
2 bars (8 oz.) Ghirardelli Bittersweet Chocolate baking bars, broken into ¼" pieces
6 T. unsalted butter, cut into small pieces
1/3 c. Ghirardelli unsweetened cocoa

In a small saucepan, bring the cream to a simmer. Remove from the heat, and stir in the chocolate and butter. In a medium-sized skillet, bring ½" water to a slow simmer. Set the saucepan in the skillet over low heat. Stir mixture just until chocolate has completely melted. Remove from heat. Pour the chocolate mixture into a shallow bowl. Cool, cover and refrigerate until firm, at least 2 hours. Pour the cocoa into a pie plate. Line an airtight container with waxed paper. Dip a melon baller or small spoon into a glass of warm water and quickly scrape across the surface of the chilled truffle mixture to form a rough 1" ball. Drop the ball into the cocoa. Repeat with the remaining truffle mixture. Gently shake the pie plate to coat truffles evenly. Transfer truffles to the prepared container, separating layers with additional waxed paper. Cover tightly and refrigerate up to two weeks or freeze up to three months. Makes 30 truffles.

CARAMEL TRUFFLES

26 caramels
1 c. milk chocolate chips
¼ c. heavy whipping cream
1-1/3 c. semisweet chocolate chips
1 T. shortening

Line an 8" square dish with plastic wrap and set aside. In a microwave-safe bowl, combine the caramels, milk chocolate chips and cream. Microwave, uncovered, on high for 1 minute; stir. Microwave 1 minute longer, stirring every 15 seconds or until caramels are melted and mixture is smooth. Spread into prepared dish; refrigerate for 1 hour or until firm.

Using plastic wrap, lift candy out of pan. Cut into 30 pieces; roll each piece into a 1" ball. Cover and refrigerate for 1 hour or until firm.

In a microwave-safe bowl, melt semi-sweet chips and shortening; stir until smooth. Dip caramels in chocolate and place on waxed paper-lined baking sheets. Refrigerate until firm. Yield: 2½ dozen.

BUTTERSCOTCH HARD CANDY

2½ c. sugar
¾ c. water
½ c. light corn syrup
1 c. butter, cubed
¼ c. honey
½ tsp. salt
½ tsp. rum extract

Butter a 15" x 10" x 1" baking pan; set aside. In a heavy saucepan, combine the sugar, water and corn syrup. Cover and bring to a boil over medium heat without stirring. Cook, uncovered, until a candy thermometer reads 270 degrees (soft-crack stage). Add the butter, honey, salt and extract; stir constantly until the mixture reaches 300 degrees (hard-crack stage).

Remove from the heat. Pour into prepared pan without scraping; do not spread. Cool for 1-2 minutes or until the candy is almost set. Score into 1" squares; cool completely. Break squares apart. Store in an airtight container. Yield: 1½ pounds.

HOLIDAY FUDGE
Combine in a large mixing bowl and set aside:
1 c. (6 oz.) semisweet chocolate chips
1 c. chopped walnuts
1 tsp. vanilla
½ c. (1 stick) butter

Combine in a saucepan:
12 large marshmallows (no mini's, no marshmallow cream)
2 c. granulated sugar
¾ c. evaporated milk

Bring the ingredients in the saucepan to a boil over medium-high heat and then turn the heat down to medium so the mixture continues to boil actively, stirring constantly. Once the marshmallows melt, continue boiling and stirring for exactly 6 minutes (time this carefully) and remove from stove. Immediately pour this hot liquid over ingredients in the bowl. Stir to combine and then beat by hand for exactly 20 minutes (you may also do this with an electric mixer set on "low") or until you cannot stir it any longer because it is so thick. Pour into a lightly buttered 8" square glass dish. Hint: Spray the pan with nonstick baking spray to make sure the fudge comes out easily.) Sprinkle a few ground nuts on top (optional) and refrigerate to harden. Wait for several hours, and then cut into squares.

"I signed up for an exercise class and was told to wear loose-fitting clothing. If I HAD any loose-fitting clothing, I wouldn't have signed up in the first place!"

HOLIDAY HASH
3 c. Rice Chex
3 c. Corn Chex
3 c. Cheerios
2 c. small pretzels
2 c. salted peanuts
1 (12 oz.) bag plain M & M's
1 (12 oz.) bag peanut M & M's
2 (12 oz.) bags of white chocolate chips

continued...

HOLIDAY HASH continued...

Combine all of the ingredients except the white chocolate chips in a big bowl. Melt the white chocolate chips in a saucepan according to the package instructions. These chips burn quickly, so be careful to not overcook them. Pour the melted white chocolate over the mixture and with a strong long-handled wooden spoon, toss well to coat.

Spread the Holiday Hash out on waxed paper and let set until the chocolate hardens. Break the hash into palm-sized pieces and store them in an airtight container or pour into gift bags. Hint: If you buy the red and green M & M's you will have a very festive result.

HOW TO SPEAK ABOUT MEN AND BE POLITICALLY CORRECT:

*He does not have a beer gut,
he has developed a grain alcohol
storage facility.*

*He is not a bad dancer,
he is overly caucasian.*

*He does not get lost all the time,
he investigates Alternative.*

December 18, 1913 – Still no snow, and little frost in the ground. This is the latest season in Minnesota since the winter of 1877 when the Journal editor, who resided in Big Stone County this state, stopped plowing Christmas Eve. In the following spring much of the grain was sown in February while the ice on that lake went out on March 14. The lake usually clears about May 1. ... *Bear River Journal* **courtesy of Gloria Anderson Hegg.**

Desserts

Dad, Grandpa's brother Edwin Williams
from Rapid City SD, Grandpa Williams,
Joe Kitchen (Santa Claus)

BAKED ALASKA

I always asked for this for my birthday party. The kids were wowed over by this great dessert! They thought my mom was the greatest cook.

½ yellow cake
8 egg whites
¼ tsp. cream of tartar
½ granulated sugar
½ gallon any flavor ice cream you desire

Prepare cake recipe as directed. Pour batter into greased 9" square cake pan; bake as directed. Remove from pan; cool. Cut in half horizontally.
Hint: use thread to cut cake apart. Place ½ of cake on heatproof platter.
Beat egg whites until foamy. Add cream of tartar; mix in. Add sugar gradually, continuing to beat until egg whites form stiff peaks.

Remove ice cream from container. Place on cake and put the other half of cake on top of ice cream. Cover generously with meringue; be sure to smooth and cover entire surface. You can decorate the meringue, working quickly, by filling a pastry bag with meringue. Place in preheated 400 degree oven 3 minutes or until meringue just begins to turn brown. Serve immediately. Serves 18.

"Time may be a great healer, but it is a lousy beautician."
"Forget the health food. I need all the preservatives I can get."

GRAPES IN SOUR CREAM WITH BROWN SUGAR

5 heaping c. seedless grapes
1-1/2 c. sour cream
½ c. brown sugar

Wash and chill grapes. Pluck grapes from stems so that all used are perfect. Have both grapes and cream very cold.

Mix grapes with cream and place in silver or glass bowl. Chill again. Sprinkle sugar over entire top just before serving. Sugar may be sieved or dropped in lumps if you like that effect. Serve with a thin, crisp spice cookie.

Serves 6.

CHOCOLATE BREAD PUDDING WITH IRISH CREAM SAUCE

SAUCE:
2 c. whipping cream
6 T. Irish cream liqueur
¼ c. sugar
½ tsp. vanilla extract
2 tsp. cornstarch
2 tsp. water

BREAD PUDDING:
14 c. ¾" cubes French bread with crust (about 12 oz.)
6 oz. bittersweet (not unsweetened) or semisweet chocolate, chopped
6 oz. imported white chocolate, chopped
4 large eggs
½ c. plus 4 T. sugar
2 tsp. vanilla extract
2 c. whipping cream
½ c. whole milk
Nonstick vegetable oil spray

FOR SAUCE: Bring cream, liqueur, sugar, and vanilla to boil in heavy medium saucepan over medium-high heat, stirring frequently. Mix cornstarch and 2 tsp. water in small bowl to blend; whisk into cream mixture. Boil until sauce thickens, stirring constantly, about 3 minutes. Cool, then cover and refrigerate until cold, about 2 hours. Can be made 3 days ahead. Keep refrigerated.

FOR BREAD PUDDING: Combine bread, chocolate, and white chocolate in large bowl; toss to blend. Using electric mixer, beat eggs, ½ c. plus 4 T. sugar. Add eggs, vanilla extract, whipping cream and whole milk and mix well. Spray 13 x 9 x 2" casserole with nonstick vegetable oil spray. Put bread cubes and chocolate in casserole. Add egg mixture and let set for 15 to 30 minutes. Put casserole in larger pan and pour boiling water into pan until 1" deep. Bake uncovered 40 to 45 minutes at 350 degrees until knife inserted 1" from edge of casserole comes out clean. Warm sauce and pour over.

A MESSAGE FROM NORTHERN MINNESOTA....
"It's called a 'gravel road'. No matter how slow you drive, you're going to get dust on your Navigator. I have a four-wheel drive because I need it. Drive it or get it out of my way."

CHOCOLATE TRIFLE
For all of you chocolate lovers out there.

1 box chocolate cake mix
½ c. coffee liqueur
2 c. fudge sauce
2 chocolate covered toffee candy bars, broken into pieces
1-1/2 c. heavy cream whipped and sweetened with 1/3 cup sugar

Prepare the cake according to the package directions for a 9 x 13" cake. Cool thoroughly.

Prick the entire top of the cake with a fork. Pour coffee liqueur over the cake and allow it to soak in. Wrap the cake with plastic and refrigerate for at least three hours. Slice the cake into 1" thick pieces.

Line the bottom of a large glass bowl with a single layer of cake. Pour ¼ of the fudge sauce over the cake, top with ¼ of the candy bar-bits then 1/3 of the whipped cream. Repeat layering two more times ending with fudge sauce and candy bits. Refrigerate until ready to serve.

Assemble the trifle shortly before serving or it will get soggy.

CHERRY ANGEL FOOD TRIFLE
5 c. angel food cake cubes
¼ c. cherry liqueur
1 c. confectioner's sugar
1 pkg. (3 oz.) cream cheese, softened
1 carton (8 oz.) frozen whipped topping, thawed, divided
½ c. toasted chopped pecans
1 can (21 oz.) cherry pie filling

Place the cake cubes in large bowl. Sprinkle with liqueur if desired; let stand 30 minutes. In a medium bowl, combine confectioner's sugar and cream cheese; beat until blended. Reserve 2 tablespoons whipped topping; fold remaining topping into cheese mixture. Stir topping mixture and pecans into cake cubes; mix well. Spoon cake mixture into a trifle dish or a deep salad bowl. Spread cherry filling evenly over top. Or, if desired, layer one-half cake mixture and cherry filling, repeat layers. Cover; refrigerate at least 3 hours. Garnish with reserved topping. Yield: 8-10 servings.

THE BEST EVER COBBLER

This past summer, friend Margy from St. Cloud and I found this recipe and made it way too many times!

Batter:
1 c. self-rising flour or favorite baking mix
1 c. sugar
½ c. milk

Stir together all ingredients and set aside.

Fruit:
3 c. fresh fruit (or one 15 oz. can)
2/3 c. sugar
2 T. flour or baking mix
1 stick of butter or margarine

Preheat oven to 350 degrees. Melt butter in a 9 x 13" baking dish. Toss together fruit, sugar, and baking mix. Pour batter into baking dish. Spoon fruit mixture over the top. Bake 30 to 40 minutes or until the batter is golden and fruit is bubbly. Serve warm with ice cream.

COTTAGE CHEESE CREPES WITH ALMONDS

Buy ready made crepes from your grocery store.

¼ c. plus 2 T. sliced almonds
1 c. (8 oz.) low-fat whipped cottage cheese
2 T. sugar
½ tsp. ground cinnamon
4 store-bought crepes (6"), room temperature sliced in half crosswise
2 T. apricot jam

Preheat oven to 350 degrees with rack in center. Spread almonds in a single layer on a baking sheet; bake until golden brown, about 8 minutes. Let cool slightly. Reserve 2 T. for garnish.

In a medium bowl, stir together cottage cheese, sugar, and cinnamon. Stir in almonds. Dollop 2 T. cheese mixture on the short end of each crepe half, carefully roll into a tight cylinder. If you can't find whipped cottage cheese, use low-fat variety in the same amount and place in the food processor and blend until smooth.

continued...

COTTAGE CHEESE CREPES WITH ALMONDS continued...

Place crepes, seam side down and 1" apart, on a baking sheet. Bake until warmed through and beginning to brown on edges, about 5 minutes.

Meanwhile, heat jam and 2 T. water in a small saucepan over medium heat (or in the microwave) until jam is liquefied; whisk to combine. Transfer 2 crepes to each of four plates and drizzle with apricot sauce; sprinkle with reserved almonds. Serve immediately.

CREAM PUFFS WITH A LEMON TWIST

Dad loved when mom made cream puffs – we all did. Of course, they were filled with sweetened whipping cream. This recipe has a lemon zest.

Cream Puffs:
½ c. water
¼ c. butter (no substitutes), cubed
½ c. all-purpose flour
2 eggs

Lemon Filling:
1 egg, beaten
1/3 c. sugar
3 T. lemon juice
2 T. butter, cubed
1 c. heavy whipping cream
2 tsp. sugar
Confectioners' sugar

IIn a saucepan, bring water and butter to a boil. Add flour all at once, stirring until a smooth ball forms. Remove from the heat; let stand for 5 minutes. Add eggs, one at a time, beating well after each addition. Continue beating until mixture is smooth.

Drop by rounded tablespoonfuls 3" apart onto greased baking sheets. Bake at 400 degrees for 30 to 35 minutes or until golden brown. Remove to wire racks. Immediately split puffs and remove tops; discard soft dough from inside. Set puffs and tops aside to cool.

For filling, in a small heavy saucepan, combine the egg, sugar, lemon juice and butter. Bring to a boil over medium heat; cook and stir for 5-7

continued...

CREAM PUFFS WITH A LEMON TWIST continued....
minutes or until mixture is thick enough to coat a metal spoon.

 Remove from heat. Cool quickly by placing pan in a bowl of ice water; stir for 2 minutes. Transfer to a bowl; press plastic wrap onto surface of filling. Chill for 1 hour or until partially set.

IIn a mixing bowl, beat cream and sugar until stiff peaks form; fold into lemon mixture. Fill cream puffs; replace tops. Dust with confectioners' sugar. 10 servings.

FROZEN LEMON YOGURT

1 carton (32 oz.) plain yogurt
1-2/3 c. sugar
1/3 c. lemon juice
1 T. grated lemon peel
4 drops yellow food coloring, optional

In a mixing bowl, combine the yogurt, sugar, lemon juice and peel; mix well. Stir in food coloring if desired. Fill cylinder of ice cream freezer 2/3 full; freeze according to the manufacturer's directions. Refrigerate remaining mixture until ready to freeze. Allow to ripen in ice cream freezer or firm up in the refrigerator freezer for at least 2-4 hours before serving.   Yield: 5 cups.

Minnesota Temperature Chart:
"At 50 degrees: North Carolinians
turn on their heat full-blast.
Minnesotans sit out in the sun."

ENGLISH TRIFLE

How my Finnish father loved this recipe. My mother always made this on Christmas Eve.

Sponge cake (buy one)
2/3 c. medium sherry
1 large pkg. (5-1/2 oz.) vanilla instant pudding
2-1/2 c. milk
1 c. light cream
1 qt. fresh or frozen whole strawberries, sliced or raspberries
½ c. sliced almonds
½ c. whipping cream
1T. Confectioners sugar
1/3 tsp. sherry flavor

Cut cake into small pieces (about 36). Place on baking sheet. Sprinkle with sherry. Let stand 15 minutes. Prepare pudding according to package directions using milk and light cream. Let stand 5 minutes. Arrange a layer of cake pieces in bottom of 2-1/2 or 3 quart serving bowl. Top with 1/3 of the sliced strawberries. Spread about 1-1/3 cup pudding over strawberries. Sprinkle with 1/3 of the almonds. Make two more complete layers. Refrigerate two hours or until thoroughly chilled. Whip cream, sugar and sherry flavor in small bowl. Garnish with shipped cream and whole strawberries. Serves 12. Spectacular in a deep-sided crystal bowl.

"The problem with the designated driver program, it's not a desirable job, but if you ever get sucked into doing it, have fun with it. At the end of the night, drop them off at the wrong house."
Jeff Foxworthy

GOOEY CHOCOLATE-CARAMEL DESSERT
Boy this is low calorie!

2 c. chocolate wafer crumbs (about 38 wafers)
1/3 c. butter, melted
30 vanilla caramels
½ c. caramel ice cream topping
¼ c. whipping cream
2 c. chopped pecans
¾ c. semisweet chocolate pieces
¼ c. whipping cream

In a medium mixing bowl, stir together chocolate wafer crumbs and melted butter. Press onto the bottom of a 9" spring form pan. Bake in a 350 degree oven for 10 minutes. Cool slightly on a wire rack.

In a heavy medium saucepan, melt caramels in caramel ice cream topping over low heat, stirring often. Stir in the first 1/4 c. whipping cream. Remove from heat; stir in nuts. Spread over crust. Cool; cover and chill for one hour.

For topping: In a heavy small saucepan, melt chocolate. Remove from heat; stir in remaining whipping cream.

Drizzle or spread over caramel-pecan mixture. Cover and chill for at least one hour. Makes 12 servings.

ELLO ORANGE WEDGES
The kids will love these but make sure you leave out the vodka. The big kids REALLY like them!!

2 navel oranges
Juice from the two oranges
1 envelope (1 T. unflavored gelatin)
1-1/2 oz. vodka

Cut the oranges in half crosswise and squeeze out the juice. Strain and measure. You should have about 1-3/4 cups juice. Add more juice if you have less than this amount. Carefully scrape out and discard the pulp from the two navel oranges to form half shells. Combine ¼ cup of the juice and the gelatin in a small saucepan. Set aside for 5 minutes to dissolve the gelatin. Heat the mixture slowly over low heat and stir constantly until smooth, 3 to 4 minutes. Whisk in the remaining juice and the vodka. Arrange the orange shells cut side up in muffin tins. Divide the mixture among the 4 shells and cover each with plastic wrap. Chill until firm, at least 4 hours and preferably overnight. Cut each half into 3 wedges before serving.

RASPBERRY BREAD PUDDING
4 c. 2" cubes day old bread (5 to 7 slices)
1 c. fresh raspberries
½ c. raisins, optional
2-1/2 c. low-fat milk
2 eggs, slightly beaten
2 T. packed brown sugar
1 tsp. vanilla
½ tsp. ground cinnamon
¼ tsp. ground nutmeg

Heat oven to 350 degrees. Spray square baking dish, 8x8x2", with nonstick cooking spray. Mix all ingredients; let stand 15 minutes. Spread mixture in baking dish. Place baking dish in rectangular pan, 13x9x2", on oven rack. Pour boiling water into pan until 1" deep. Bake 25 to 30 minutes or until brown.

DIET BERRIES DESSERT
16 oz. carton lowfat plain yogurt
4 T. maple syrup
1 carton washed blueberries
1 carton washed raspberries
If not dieting, brown sugar for syrup and sour cream for yogurt.

Beat 4T. of maple syrup into 16 oz. of yogurt in a bowl. Fold in the blueberries and raspberries gently, then refrigerate at least one hour. This is a refreshing for the diet-conscious who like to finish their meal with a dessert.

From the Bear River Journal .....October 19, 1912

"Mr. and Mrs. Rhodes of the Orpheum Theater at Hibbing were in the village Tuesday, bringing Mrs. E. E. Pixley who has been in that place for several days. This was their first trip and made the distance, 28 miles, in an hour and 28 minutes."
(Thanks to Gloria Anderson Hegg)

MOM'S HOT FUDGE

Forgot to put this one in the other cookbook.

1 c. sugar
1/3 c. milk – evaporated, not sweetened
2 T. white Karo syrup
2 T. cocoa
¼ c. butter

Boil for 2 minutes, stir constantly. Add 1 tsp. vanilla.

CREAMY FROSTING

Just two ingredients and can be spread on cupcakes or between cookies.

Using an electric mixer, beat 3 ounces softened reduced-fat cream cheese and 1 cup confectioners' sugar until light and fluffy.

Can be refrigerated in an airtight container for up to one week.

RECIPE FOR HAPPINESS

*1 funny bone
1 big smile
1 big handful of patience
Dash of courtesy*

Mix with humility and love, put through a sieve to strain out all unkindness. Serve to everyone you meet.

Breads
Quick/Yeast

**Cousin Jack Williams
and Brother Roger**

"CHEESE BISCUITS from you know where"

1-1/4 lb. (about 4 plus cups) Bisquick
3 oz. shredded cheddar cheese
1-1/3 c. cold water

Garlic spread:
½ c. melted butter
1 tsp. garlic powder
¼ tsp. salt
1/8 tsp. onion powder
1/8 tsp. dried parsley

To cold water, add Bisquick and cheese, blending in a mixing bowl. Mix until dough is firm. Using a small scoop, place the dough on a baking pan lined with baking paper. Bake in 375 degree oven for 10 to 12 minutes or until golden brown. While biscuits bake, combine spread ingredients. Brush baked biscuits with the garlic topping.

GREAT TASTING CORN BREAD

1 c. Bisquick
1 c. cornmeal
2 T. sugar, if desired
½ tsp. salt
1 c. milk
¼ c. vegetable oil
2 eggs
1 pkg. (4 oz.) shredded sharp Cheddar cheese (1 cup)
2/3 c. frozen whole kernel corn, thawed and drained
2 T. canned diced green chilies
Great Tasting Corn Bread continued....

Heat oven to 400 degrees. Spray with cooking spray or grease bottom of 9" square pan. Stir Bisquick mix, cornmeal, sugar, salt, milk, oil and eggs in medium bowl just until moistened. Gently stir in remaining ingredients. Pour into pan. Bake 28 to 32 minutes or until light brown. Serve warm.

BEER BREAD
Great for the deer camp....

3 c. self-rising flour
½ c. sugar
  Optional: 2 tsp. Italian seasoning
            2 tsp. garlic powder
            2 T. parmesan cheese
12 oz. can beer

Preheat oven to 375 degrees. Grease loaf pan. In large bowl, combine dry ingredients and beer. Mix well. The mixture will be sticky. Pour into loaf pan. Bake for 55 minutes. Last 3 minutes of baking, brush top of loaf with 2 T. melted butter. Return to oven.

POPOVERS
1 c. flour
½ tsp. salt
2 eggs
1 c. milk

Preheat oven to 425 degrees. Grease 6 large muffin tins or ovenproof custard cups. Place on baking sheet in oven to heat thoroughly just before filling. Measure all ingredients into a bowl and beat until mixture is very smooth. It is a thin batter. Fill cups a little less than half full and bake 30 minutes without peeking, or until sides are rigid to the touch. If drier popovers are desired, pierce each one with knife and bake 5 minutes longer.

According to Dinah Shore the three tricks are the preheated custard cups or muffin tins, filling them less than half full of batter so the popovers will have room to grown, and not peeking.

"Do you know why they call it "PMS"? Because "Mad Cow Disease" was taken." - Unknown, presumed deceased.

HAM AND CHEESE MUFFINS

2 eggs
3 c. Bisquick
1 c. milk
3 T. vegetable oil
1 pkg. (4 oz. shredded Cheddar cheese – 1 cup)
¾ c. chopped fully cooked ham (about ¼ pound)

Heat oven to 400 degrees. Spray bottoms and sides of 12 muffin cups with cooking spray. Beat eggs slightly in medium bowl with fork. Stir in Bisquick mix, milk and oil. Stir in ¾ c. of cheese and the ham. Divide batter evenly among muffin cups. Sprinkle remaining ¼ c. cheese over tops of muffins. Bake 18 to 20 minutes. Immediately

COTTAGE CHEESE STRUDEL

Mary Ann Stanich's recipe – this was inadvertently omitted in the last cookbook. This is my favorite!

Dough:

3 c. flour   ½ tsp. salt
½ c. oil less 2 T.   1 egg
¾ c. warm water

Use fork for mixing. Knead until stiff or fat comes out – about 15 minutes. Roll out with rolling pin to fit oiled pan. Let set for 1 hour.

Filling:

2 lb. cottage cheese
5 eggs
Salt
Add together:
2 c. sugar sprinkled in cottage cheese
1 c. butter

When ready to make cheese roll, cover a table with a cloth or sheet. Sprinkle well with flour and pat flour into cloth. Place dough in center of table and brush well with melted butter. Next pull dough from all sides until very thin. Begin pulling gently, with one hand on top and one underneath. Some cooks use a rolled fist or the top of the hand underneath. Work from the center outward, walking around table and pulling on all sides until dough is 8 ft.x 6 ft. (yes, you got that right – you need a big table) or try half of recipe for smaller version.

continued...

COTTAGE CHEESE STRUDEL continued...

Spread cheese mixture along 6 ft. side. Leave about 10 inches at far end of rectangle free of filling for a better seal. Cut edges of dough on table with knife. After starting rolling by hand, the edge of cloth can be raised and dough will gently roll over on top of itself. When rolled, pinch ends and edge of roll well. Put in 9 x 13 pan. Drizzle butter on entire dough. Bake ½ hour or until golden brown at 375 degrees.

Filling for apple strudel:
1 c. graham cracker or corn flake crumbs
1 c. brown sugar
1 c. white sugar
1 tsp. cinnamon
Make dough apple same as cottage cheese strudel.
GOOD LUCK!

CHOCOLATE CHIP SCONES

2 c. Bisquick mix
1/3 c. whipping (heavy) cream
1 egg
Additional whipping (heavy) cream

½ c. semisweet chocolate chips
3 T. sugar
1 tsp. vanilla
Additional sugar

Heat oven to 425 degrees. Spray with cooking spray or grease cookie sheet. Stir Bisquick mix, chocolate chips, 1/3 c. whipping cream, 3T. sugar, the egg and vanilla until soft dough forms.

Pat into 8" circle on cookie sheet (if dough is sticky, dip fingers in Bisquick). Brush circle with additional whipping cream; sprinkle with additional sugar. Cut into 8 wedges, but do not separate.

Bake about 12 minutes or until golden brown; carefully separate. Serve warm. 8 scones.

Raisin Scones: Omit chocolate chips and vanilla; add ½ c. raisins. Drizzle warm scones with mixture of ½ c. powdered sugar and 1T. whipping cream.

Drop Scones: Heat oven to 400 degrees. Drop dough into 8 mounds onto cookie sheet; pat to slightly flatten. Bake 10 to 12 minutes or until golden brown.

"24 hours in a day, 24 beers in a case. Coincidence? I think not." —Stephen Wright

BUN-STEADS
Big for Friday nights after an athletic contest at the Retica house

¼ pound American cheese (1 c. cubed)
3 hard cooked eggs, chopped
1-7 oz. can tuna, flaked
2 T. chopped green pepper
2 T. stuffed olives
2 T. chopped sweet pickle
½ c. mayo or salad dressing
6 hot dog buns

Combine all, mix lightly. Fill buns. Wrap buns in aluminum foil. Place in 250 degree slow oven for about 30 minutes. Makes 6 generously or 8 if not as full.

SANDWICH LOAVES
This was served at wedding showers, baby showers and they still make it at Sunrise Bakery. How I love this!

1 loaf uncut bread, remove all crust from bread; and cut lengthwise into 4 equally thick slices.

Butter each length of bread and spread one length with ham salad, one with chicken salad, one with egg salad. Other variations can be used.

Place reshaped loaf onto serving platter; spread top and sides with thick layer of cream cheese that has been softened with a little cream or milk. Decorate top as you wish. Refrigerate 3 to 4 hours; cut through in slices. Serves 7 or 8.

THE NEW 60'S SONGS
Some of the artists of the 60's are revising their hits with new lyrics to accommodate aging baby boomers. They include:

Herman's Hermit's – "Mrs. Brown, You've Got a Lovely Walker"
Ringo Starr – "I Get By With a Little Help from Depends"
The Bee Gees – "How Can You Mend a Broken Hip"
Marvin Gaye – "I Heard it Through the Grape Nuts"
Helen Reddy – "I am Woman, Hear me Snore"
Willy Nelson – "On the Throne Again"

SWISS CHEESE BREAD

Heat 1/3 c. butter and 1 c. milk until butter is melted:

Beat in ¼ tsp. salt and 1 c. flour.

Beat in 4 eggs one at a time; beating constantly. Remove pan from heat after each addition.

Remove from heat and blend in:

½ c. grated or shredded Swiss cheese
1/8 tsp. dry mustard
½ tsp. minced onion

Mound on 10" sprayed pie plate. Sprinkle 3 T. grated Swiss cheese on top
Bake at 375 degrees for 20 minutes, then reduce to 350 degrees and bake for 20 minutes. Serve hot.

PARMESAN WAFERS

Blend well:
1½ c. grated parmesan cheese
1 c. flour
½ c. butter, room temperature
¾ tsp. oregano
½ tsp. marjoram
½ tsp. basil

Add:
½ tsp. Worcestershire sauce
3 T. dry white wine

Form into two logs approximately 1-1/2" in diameter. Wrap and refrigerate. Cut ¼" slices and place ½" apart on sprayed baking sheet. Bake 400 degrees for 12 to 15 minutes. Serve hot. Makes about 4 dozen wafers.

Mechanic to man…"I couldn't repair your brakes, so I made your horn louder."

SAUSAGE LOAVES

Mix together:

2 c. flour	3 T. grated parmesan cheese
2 T. brown sugar	1 T. sugar
1 T. baking powder	½ tsp. baking soda
½ tsp. salt	1 tsp. caraway seed

Combine:
1 c. whipped cream cheese
¾ c. milk
2 eggs, one at a time
2 T. butter, melted
1 c. crumbled or chopped sausage*
*Pepperoni or fresh sausage, crumbled and stir fried until crisp and then drained.

Combine mixtures until just moistened and spoon into 3 sprayed 8 x 4 loaf pans. Bake at 375 degrees for 45 to 50 minutes.

Yeast

DINNER ROLLS – THE EASY WAY

1 c. warm water
2 pkgs. active dry yeast
½ c. butter, melted
½ c. sugar
3 eggs
1 tsp. salt
4 to 4-1/2 c. unbleached all-purpose flour
Additional melted butter (optional)
Makes 2 dozen rolls

Combine the warm water and yeast in a large bowl. Let the mixture stand until yeast is foamy, about 5 minutes.

Stir in butter, sugar, eggs and salt. Beat in flour, 1 cup at a time until dough is too stiff to mix (some flour may not be needed). Cover and refrigerate 2 hours or up to 4 days.

Grease 13 x 9 inch baking pan. Turn the chilled dough out onto a lightly floured board. Divide dough into 24 equal-size pieces. Roll each piece into a smooth round ball; place balls in even rows in the prepared pan. Cover and let dough balls rise until doubled in volume, about 1 hour.

continued...

DINNER ROLLS – THE EASY WAY continued...

Preheat over to 375 degrees. Bake until rolls are golden brown, 15 to 20 minutes. Brush warm rolls with melted butter, if desired. Break rolls apart to serve

ITALIAN SWEET BREAD

Make this in your bread machine.

1 c. warm milk (70 to 80 degrees)
1 egg, beaten
2 T. butter, softened
¼ c. sugar
1 tsp. salt
3 c. all-purpose flour
2 tsp. active dry yeast
Egg Wash:
1 egg
1 T. water
Italian seasoning, optional

In bread machine pan, place the first seven ingredients in order suggested by manufacturer. Select dough setting (check dough after 5 minutes of mixing; add 1 to 2 T. of water or flour if needed).

When the cycle is completed, (only finished raising) turn dough onto a floured surface. Divide in half. Shape each portion into a ball; flatten slightly. Place in two greased 9" round baking pans. Cover and let rise until doubled, about 45 minutes.

Beat egg and water; brush over the dough. Sprinkle with Italian seasoning if desired. Bake at 350 degrees for 20-25 minutes or until golden brown. Remove from pans to wire racks to cool. Yield: 2 loaves (3/4 pound each).

"July 2, 1914...Adolph Swanson of Bearville autoed over to Hibbing and returned today. This is a great improvement over the old time trip which required from a week to ten days."
Bear River Journal

LOW-CARB PIZZA DOUGH
Probably two carbs less…

¼ oz. yeast
½ tsp. honey
1 c. warm water
2¼ c. all-purpose flour
1 tsp. salt
4 tsp. olive oil

In a small bowl, dissolve the yeast and honey in ¼ c. of the warm water. In a mixer fitted with a dough hook, combine the flour and the salt. Add the oil, yeast mixture and the remaining ¾ c. of water and mix on low speed.

Form dough into 2-1/2 oz. balls. With a floured rolling pin, roll out the dough to form 8" rounds.

RUSTIC ITALIAN BREAD
Very tasty…..

1 c. water heated to 120 to 130 degrees
2 T. olive oil
3 c. bread flour
2 tsp. sugar
½ tsp. salt
1 pkg. active dry yeast
Cornmeal
1 egg white, beaten

Bread Machine Directions: Place all ingredients except cornmeal and egg white in bread machine pan according to directions. Process on dough setting.

Sprinkle ungreased cookie sheet with cornmeal. At the end of dough cycle, remove dough from machine; place on lightly floured surface. Punch down dough. If dough is sticky, knead in additional flour before shaping. Cover dough with clean cloth; let rest for 15 minutes. Shape dough into baguette-shaped loaf about 12" long. Place loaf on cornmeal-coated sheet. Cover; let rise in warm place for 30 to 35 minutes or until light and doubled in size.

Heat oven to 375 degrees. With sharp knife, make one deep lengthwise slash in top of loaf. Brush loaf with egg white. Bake at 375 degrees for 25 to 35 minutes or until loaf sounds hollow when lightly tapped. One loaf of bread.

LAZY MAN'S BBQ PORK SANDWICHES

My sister-in-law Tammi Meittunen makes this for my brother Mark. The men in our family don't cook much. Very good!

4-5 lb. boneless pork butt (shoulder)
1- (14.5 oz.) can beef broth
1/3 c. hot pepper sauce
1/3 c. Worcestershire sauce

Sauce:
½ c. catsup
½ c. molasses
¼ c. Worcestershire sauce
¼ c. yellow mustard
2 T. hot pepper sauce

10-12 sandwich buns

Place pork butt in bottom of large slow cooker. Combine broth, hot pepper sauce and Worcestershire sauce and pour over pork. Cover and cook on hot setting for 5 hours (or 8-10 hours on low setting) until pork is very tender.

Meanwhile, for sauce, combine all ingredients in large saucepan; set aside.

Place pork on cutting board; reserve ½ cup cooking liquid.

Coarsely chop pork; combine with reserved cooking liquid and sauce in saucepan; heat over medium heat until warm.

Spoon pork onto sandwich buns to serve.

Insomnia? Eat honey!
Use honey as a tranquilizer and sedative.

OLD FASHIONED HAM SALAD
Terry Backstrom's favorite!

1 package bologna
2 dill pickles
1 onion
Miracle Whip

Grind bologna, pickles and onion in meat grinder. Fold in Miracle Whip. Serve on bread to make sandwich.

CORNED BEEF SANDWICH
1 can corned beef, shredded
1 c. cheddar cheese, shredded
½ c. stuffed olives, chopped
½ c. catsup
¼ c. onion, minced
2 T. Worcestershire sauce

Mix together. Put between 12 buns. Wrap in foil; bake at 350 degrees for 20 minutes. Make ahead and freeze.

OPEN-FACED SANDWICHES
1 can Spam
¼ lb. cheese
1 small onion
1 can cream of mushroom soup

Grind meat, cheese, and onion. Add mushroom soup. Spread on half hamburger bun and broil for a few minutes.

"Pain: A cat licking your sunburn."

Pancakes
Eggs

Durwood Oothoudt
Story on Page 151

APPLE PANCAKES

My brother-in-law Ron Sundquist made these for me one morning in White Bear Lake. I was truly amazed and ate with gusto!

Combine ½ c. sugar and 1T. cinnamon – set aside.

1 egg
1 T. olive oil
1 c. milk
1 c. flour
½ tsp. baking soda
Or use premixed pancake dough

Apples, butter, almonds and whipping cream are also needed.

Make batter (this amount will make about 4 to 5 pancakes).

Peel and cut apples lengthwise, core. Slice apples lengthwise with a thickness of 1/8". Heat pan and add oil. Place the apple slices in a circle in pan. Heat slices for 30 seconds to soften. Pour batter over slices and cover slices completely.

Now comes the hard part – flipping pancakes.

Flip pancakes when they bubble in pan. Take pan from stove. Place spatula under pancake. Give a quick upward motion of pan and spatula and flip.

Butter pancake in pan. When on a plate, sprinkle sugar/cinnamon mixture, add slivered almonds and top with whipped cream.

"If I Can't Be Number One In Your Life,
Then Number Two On You."
Country Western Song

APPLE STUFFED FRENCH TOAST

Wes Millis of Makinen, MN gave me this recipe.

Filling:
2 apples
1 T. sugar
½ tsp. cinnamon
1/3 c. water

8 slices frozen bread
3 large eggs
½ c. milk
¼ tsp. cinnamon

Peel, core and thinly slice apples. In a saucepan with the water, sugar and cinnamon, cook until apples are tender. While apples are cooking spread frozen bread with cream cheese (cream cheese spreads better on frozen bread).

Layer cooked apples onto 4 slices of bread, cheese side. Top with other slices, cheese side in.

In a shallow pan mix eggs, milk and cinnamon. Place stuffed bread into mixture soaking both sides. Cook in frying pan until golden brown.

Serve with your favorite toppings.

We all started hunting and fishing when we were seven years old.
Yeah, we saw Bambi. We got over it.

BREAKFAST CASSEROLE
Great for company.

Brown 12-oz. pork sausage until thoroughly cooked, drain fat.   Add ¾ c. each chopped onion and bell pepper, and sliced fresh mushrooms. Cook until tender. Place 12 frozen biscuits in greased 13 x9-inch glass baking dish. Spoon sausage mixture over biscuits. Pour 12 beaten eggs over top. Sprinkle with 2 cups shredded cheese. Bake at 375 degrees for 35 to 45 minutes or until biscuits are done.

HASH BROWN QUICHE
24-oz. fresh hash browns (in refrigerator section)

1/3 c. melted butter	¼ c. diced onion
¼ c. diced green pepper	1 c. diced ham
4 eggs	1/3 c. milk
¼ tsp. salt	¼ tsp. pepper
1 c. shredded cheese	

In a large bowl, mix melted butter and hash browns. Press into a 9-inch pie plate. Bake at 425 degrees for 25 minutes. Sauté onion and peppers. Mix together ham, onion, peppers and cheese. Pour into baked hash browns. Beat eggs and milk and pour over top. Bake for 30 minutes more at 375 degrees or until egg is set.

RICE KRISPY QUICHE
Joyce Backstrom makes this for husband Terry.

6 c. Rice Krispies
3 pkg. Jimmy Dean sausage (brown and drain)
7 eggs (beaten)
1 c. milk
1 can cream of chicken soup
5 c. grated cheese (cheddar and mozzarella mixed together)

Mix eggs, milk, soup together. Place Rice Krispies in bottom of 9 x 13 pan. Sprinkle sausage on top of the Rice Krispies. Pour egg and milk mixture and cream of chicken soup over sausage. Top with the grated cheese.

Garnish with a couple of handfuls of Rice Krispies over the cheese. Bake at 350 degrees for 1 hour.

SPINACH-CHEESE BREAKFAST SQUARES

4 T. butter
3 eggs
1 c. flour
½ tsp. salt
1 tsp. baking powder
1 c. milk
16 oz. sharp cheddar cheese, grated
2-10 oz. pkgs. frozen spinach, thawed and well-drained

Preheat oven to 350 degrees. Melt butter in a 9 x 13" baking dish in the oven. In a large mixing bowl, beat eggs with flour; salt and baking powder. Stir in milk. Add cheese and spinach. Spread mixture Spinach-Cheese Breakfast Squares evenly in the baking dish. Bake 25 minutes or until golden and set in center. Cool and cut into squares. Can be served warm or reheated. Serves 8 to 10. Add a chopped sautéed onion with the spinach for additional zip.

MUSHROOM QUICHE

1 unbaked deep-dish pastry shell (9")
4 c. sliced fresh mushrooms
½ c. diced onion
¼ c. diced sweet red pepper
1 T. butter
1 c. (4 oz.) shredded cheddar cheese
2 T. flour
1¼ c. milk
4 eggs, lightly beaten
1 to 2 T. minced fresh savory or 1 to 2 tsp. of dried savory
1 tsp. salt
½ tsp. cayenne pepper

Line unpricked pastry shell with a double thickness of heavy-duty foil. Bake at 450 degrees for 8 minutes. Remove foil; bake 5 minutes longer. Cool on a wire rack. Reduce heat to 350 degrees.

In a large skillet, sauté the mushrooms, onion and red pepper in butter until mushrooms are tender. Drain and set aside. In a bowl, combine cheese and flour. Stir in the milk, eggs, savory, salt and cayenne until blended. Stir in mushroom mixture. Pour into crust. Bake for 40 to 50 minutes or until a knife inserted near the center comes out clean. Let stand for 10 minutes before cutting.

4-6 servings.

Pasta/Rice

Uncle Erwin Cain
1928 Pontiac

Pasta

CLAM LINGUINE
Joe Iozzo, Sr., West Sturgeon.

¼ c. olive oil
1 large onion, chopped
1 T. dried basil
2 cans baby clams, keep juice
1 can tuna or albacore in water
1 pound linguine

Sauté onion in olive oil, add rest of ingredients including juice from clams and water from tuna. Simmer for 10 to 20 minutes. Cook linguine until al dente, drain. Pour clam liquid into linguine and let it sit for 15 minutes covered.

HOMEMADE NOODLES AND ITALIAN MEATBALLS
Dick Nordvold, former mayor of Hibbing and former director of Ironworld, would make his wife's family specialty for us each Christmas. He thinks the recipe came from Papa John Rappuchi's mother Candelora Rappoccio.

MEATBALLS:
1 lb. lean ground hamburger (½ lb. hamburger with ½ lb. ground pork optional.)
1 medium onion, chopped
2 cloves fresh garlic, chopped
¼ tsp. sweet basil, crushed
¼ tsp. ground oregano
½ tsp. salt
1 T. parsley
¼ c. Italian seasoned bread crumbs
1 egg

Mix thoroughly and form into 12-16 balls. Browning is optional. (Remember the old Italians normally put the raw meatballs in the "sugo" – sauce.)

SAUCE:
2-12 oz. cans of Hunt's tomato paste (must be Hunt's)
5-12 oz. cans of water
¼ tsp. sweet basil, crushed
¼ tsp. ground oregano
1 T. parsley
1 T. chicken base (optional)

continued...

HOMEMADE NOODLES AND ITALIAN MEATBALLS continued...
¼ c. Romano cheese
Mix thoroughly making sure that paste is dissolved. Add meatballs and sausage. Simmer on low heat until sauce is of velvet consistency. Stir occasionally. Approximate time – 3 hours.

NOODLES:
2 eggs
1-1/3 c. of flour
½ tsp. salt

Mix thoroughly and knead until dough is satin in appearance and texture. Roll out noodles to desired thickness. Fold dough in thirds and cut noodles to desired width. Note: generally, allow one egg per person. Remember home made noodles take just a few minutes in boiling water.

ITALIAN POTATO GNOCCHI
This is a potato dumpling served with spaghetti sauce.

2 medium potatoes, peeled and halved
1 T. butter or margarine
1 egg yolk
1 to 1-1/4 c. all-purpose flour
Spaghetti sauce or melted butter
Grated Parmesan cheese

In a covered saucepan, cook the potatoes in enough boiling water to cover for 25 to 30 minutes or until tender. Drain off the water. In a medium mixing bowl, beat the hot potatoes, 1T. butter or margarine and 1/2 tsp. salt with an electric mixer until mixture is smooth. Add the egg yolk and 1/4 c. of the flour. Beat until smooth. Stir in as much of the remaining flour as you can with a spoon. Turn out onto a floured surface and knead in enough of the remaining flour to make a moderately stiff dough (4 to 5 minutes). With floured hands, shape dough into balls, using a scant tablespoon of dough for each ball. Crease the center of each ball with the handle of a wooden spoon. Cook gnocchi, half at a time, in a large amount of boiling salted water for four to six minutes. Using a slotted spoon, remove and drain on paper toweling. Serve with spaghetti sauce or butter and parmesan. Makes 4 servings.

"I always wake up at the crack of ice."
Joe E. Lewis, comedian

ITALIAN RICE
From my old friend Marge Ranta Radel from Chisholm

1 c. rice rinsed 6-7 times   1 lb. Italian sausage, cooked and drained
Chicken broth   Red pepper flakes (optional)

Sauté the sausage over medium heat (crumbled or cut in small pieces). Add 1 cup of rice and enough broth to moisten. Keep adding broth as it is absorbed until rice is tender and stir constantly. Add red pepper flakes and salt and pepper to taste. Sprinkle with grated Parmesan or Romano cheese. A salad tossed with vinegar and oil is enough to complete this meal.
(See her turkey low-fat sausage recipe in poultry section.)

SPAETZLE
This is a different take on the traditional German noodle.

½ lb. cooked homemade noodles (or from the store)
½ onion, minced
½ c. butter or margarine
½ c. bread crumbs
Salt to taste

Sauté onion in butter or margarine until tender. Add noodles, breadcrumbs and salt to onion mixture. Cook until golden brown stirring occasionally. Serve as a side dish instead of potatoes or with sauerkraut.

RAVIOLI IN SAFFRON CREAM SAUCE
I had this at a small Italian restaurant in Palm Springs.

They used lobster ravioli's but try chicken instead. Cook until al dente. Make sauce with heavy whipping cream, a good pinch of saffron, dash of good brandy or cognac and a little parsley. Reduce for about 15 minutes. Can add shallots.

"I go for two kinds of men.
The kind with muscles, and the kind without."
Mae West

"Instead of getting married again,
I'm going to find a woman I don't like and just give her a house."
Rod Stewart

MARSALA RED SAUCE AND MEATBALLS

Sunrise Bakery's owner Vince Forti's recipe.

1 pound noodles
4 T. olive oil
1 small onion
4 cloves crushed garlic
¾ c. Marsala or Port wine
1 tsp. plus basil, oregano, red pepper
1 tsp. salt
1 large can crushed tomatoes
1 can tomato paste and 1 can of water

Sweat garlic, onion in oil, add wine and spices. Reduce to half. Add tomatoes and ½ c. parmesan cheese (simmer).

Meatballs:
1 pound ground beef
1 small grated onion
½ c. bread crumbs
2 T. parsley
2 T. parmesan cheese
1 egg
Salt and pepper

Drop raw meatballs in into simmering sauce and cook until meat is done, usually 2 hours.

(Vince thought the Marsala wine made all the difference.)

"We lived for days on nothing but food and water."
W. C. Fields

PASTA BY MARTY IOZZO

This was an e-mail he sent to his buddies:
Hey guys, usually I don't give up my favorite recipes – I don't know what's come over me. This is kind of tricky when making multiple batches – so you'll have to keep tasting and adjusting as you go. I find beer cleanses the palate between samples. Here goes.

¾ c. olive oil
1 medium garlic bulb (yes, the whole thing) minced. Please don't use the jarred stuff.
¼ sweet onion, minced
1 pkg. sun-dried tomatoes
1 small pkg. fresh sliced mushrooms (or as many as you want)
4 to 6 shakes of dried red pepper flakes (more if you like. I like more. A lot more.)
2 to 3 pinches of kosher salt
1 pkg. of fresh basil, chopped
1 thing of broccoli (or as much as you want) Just the tops.
1 c. fresh grated romano cheese
1 pkg. (1 lb.) penne rigate

First – start the water boiling for the penne. Heat the olive oil in a large pan over medium high. Soak the tomatoes in hot water to soften.
Next – add the drained tomatoes, pepper flakes and a few pinches of salt to the oil. Adjust salt and flakes as needed. (make it a little strong, because the pasta will wash it out.)
Time to – add the mushrooms and start simmering. At first the shrooms will soak up the oil, but then it seems to come back. Go ahead – nuke the broccoli for a few minutes to par cook.At this point we throw it all together. Drain the penne (duh) and mix with the stuff in the pan. Add the broccoli, basil, half of the romano and mix well. Serve with remaining romano. This makes one batch.

Now comes the tricky part. When I make more than a single batch, I don't automatically double or triple the ingredients. For instance – I made a triple batch but I didn't start with 2-1/4 cups of olive oil (yuck). And if I would have used 3 whole bulbs of garlic – well, we'd still be on the toilet. I'd say the oil, garlic and cheese can start with 1½ recommended and add from there. If you're going to make this ahead of time and keep it warm in a roaster, don't cook the pasta completely. They'll finish in the roaster. If it dries out a little, just add more oil. Call me if I've missed anything.

Anywho – you realize now that I've given you this recipe, I will have to kill you. I'm not kidding.
      Love,
        Knuckles

SPINACH FETTUCCINE A LA NEWBURG

2 egg yolks
¼ c. butter
¼ c. all-purpose flour
½ tsp. salt
¼ tsp. pepper
2 c. milk
1 T. sherry or lemon juice
2 c. cut-up cooked seafood (can use imitation)

Beat egg yolks with fork in small bowl. Melt butter in 2-quart saucepan over low heat. Stir in flour, salt and pepper. Cook over medium heat stirring constantly, until smooth and bubbly; remove from heat. Gradually stir in milk. Heat to boiling, stirring constantly. Boil and stir 1 minute. Immediately stir at least half of the hot mixture into egg yolks; stir back into hot mixture in saucepan. Boil and stir 1 minute; remove from heat. Stir in lemon juice and seafood. Heat until seafood is hot.

Serve over spinach fettuccine. Can be served in pastry shells or over biscuits.

Serves 6.

FETTUCCINE BUTTONS

By Red Buttons, comedian.

1 pound fettuccine noodles
1 pint heavy sweet cream
1 c. Parmesan cheese
1 dash vermouth
1 stick of butter (he had margarine)

Place butter in pan and melt. Boil noodles and drain. Place noodles in melted butter, put cream and cheese in pan, mix with two forks, keep stirring, add dash of Vermouth, season with garlic to taste.

Main Dishes/Meats
Beef/Pork/Venison/Spam
Fish/Shrimp/Chicken/Turkey

Dad, Brothers Roger Meittunen, Mark and Todd, 1964

Beef

WORLD FAMOUS HOT DISH
Guys – make this one at the hunting shack!

1½ lb. hamburger
¾ c. diced celery
½ medium sized onion, diced
Brown – do not season.

Add:
1 can whole kernel corn
2 cans cream of chicken soup
1 can chicken rice soup
2 generous T. soy sauce
1 (heaping) c. chow mein noodles

Mix well and bake at 350 degrees for 45-60 minutes.

Hints for your car...
Quick window cleaning – baking soda quickly cleans spatters and grime from windshields, headlights, chrome and enamel. Wipe with soda, sprinkled onto a damp sponge or dissolve 2 T. in a quart of water. Rinse.

Removing rust spots – Briskly scrub the rust spots on your bumper with a piece of foil which has been crumpled up.

Removing Road Tar – Use peanut butter to remove road tar.

Steak Doneness Rule-of-Thumb...
Professional line chefs usually rely upon the finger test to determine the doneness of steaks. Pressing quickly with forefinger or thumb...

> *A steak is rare if it gives in, exuding juices*
> *Medium if there is less give and no juices*
> *Well if there is virtually no spring and no juices*

BBQ'S

I tried this recipe from Dick (Tilly) Marinucci's cookbook. He said this was the Ting Town recipe, an old establishment on Highway 5. Although when I talked to the son of the owner (Jerry Portugue), He told me he didn't even have the recipe, that his mother had taken it to the grave. This is very good because of the amount of onions.

4 lbs. roast (pork or beef – ham can also be used)
Boil 4 hours with 1tsp. salt, 1 tsp. cloves and 1 tsp.
allspice. Save 1 cup of the water. Cool meat and shred.

Sauce:
6 T. vinegar
¼ c. lemon juice
4 medium onions, diced
2 T. prepared mustard
1 c. brown sugar
4 c. catsup
4 T. Worcestershire sauce
¼ tsp. parsley
Salt and pepper to taste

Add meat to sauce and simmer ½ hour or longer. Add meat broth if moisture is needed.

PIGS IN A BLANKET - not the sarma's!

Durwood Oothoudt's favorite recipe. Wife Eloise found this in a cookbook from The Ladies Guild of Zion Lutheran Church at Lincoln Park in Duluth, MN, November 1, 1931.

Daughter Connie relates:
This cookbook was given to me and is full of wonderful advertising including the Northland-Greyhound Lines of Hibbing, MN and the following ad:

"Duluth Ambulance Service – Not connected with any mortuary".

Method: Cut round steak into 2" strips. Place on each, a thin slice of bacon and onions (raw). Roll up and pin with a toothpick. Dredge with flour, place in a skillet and brown with drippings. Add 1 tablespoon flour, simmer in water for one hour. Serve with gravy, add salt and pepper to taste.

Beef/Pork

SPICY PEPPER STEAK

1 T. vegetable oil
¼ tsp. ground red pepper (cayenne) or a ½ tsp. red pepper sauce
1 lb. cut-up beef for stir-fry
1 med. bell pepper, cut into ¾" squares
1 medium onion, sliced
¼ c. hoisin sauce
Hot cooked noodles or rice

Heat wok or 12" skillet over high heat. Add oil and cayenne; rotate wok to coat side. Add beef; stir-fry about 2 minutes or until brown. Add pepper and onion; stir-fry about 1 minute or until vegetables are crisp. Stir in hoisin sauce; cook and stir about 30 seconds or until hot. Serve with noodles.

MADE RITES

Remember these from Malrad's Grocery on First Avenue in Hibbing? Maybe not the exact recipe, but close enough.

1 pound lean ground beef (15% fat is best)
1 c. water
¼ c. beef broth
¼ tsp. salt

Brown ground beef, drain excess fat. Add 1 cup water, beef broth and salt. Simmer for one hour or until all liquid is gone. Stir every 10 minutes.

THE BEST POT ROAST EVER...

Use a heavy sauce pot with tight fitting cover.
3 to 4 pound rump roast beef – "set aside"
Heat 2 T. olive oil in sauce pot until pan is medium hot. Add I cup coarsely chopped onion, cook until transparent. Add 4 cloves of garlic, crushed. With a slotted spoon remove onion and garlic to a small dish. Put the meat into the sauce pot, brown on all sides. Meanwhile dissolve: 2 beef bouillon cubes in one cup of hot tomato juice. When meat is browned, return the onion and garlic to the sauce pot. Add the tomato bouillon and:

1 c. red wine
½ c. chopped celery leaves
2 tsp. chopped parsley
6 whole cloves
2 bay leaves

continued...

THE BEST POT ROAST EVER... continued...

Add a mixture of: 1½ tsp. salt, ½ tsp. paprika and ¼ tsp. pepper.
Bring liquid just to boiling, stirring and scraping bottom of pot to loosen all drippings.
Reduce heat, cover and simmer (do not boil) 2½ to 3 hours or until meat is tender when pierced with a fork. Add hot water or wine if necessary.

ANOTHER POT ROAST...

Sear all sides of a 3 to 4 lb. pot roast in olive oil. Add enough water to almost cover. Add salt and pepper and 2 to 4 T. balsamic vinegar. Cover and cook on low for 2½ hours. Add potatoes, onions, baby carrots and peas and simmer another ½ hour.

JOHN DOUGHERTY'S SUGO AND POT ROAST

Here's a doozie for fast spaghetti sauce (Sugo di pomodori): In a heavy kettle, brown 6 chicken drumsticks in 2 tablespoons butter and 2 tablespoons olive oil. Add two 40 oz. jars of Ragu Traditional spaghetti sauce. Stir in a generous cup of Paisano or other mean red table wine and 2 heaping tablespoons prepared crushed garlic; a pinch of nutmeg and a pinch of ground cloves add a little piquance. Simmer slowly on stove top for two hours or pop in the oven, preheated to 325 degrees and let it go for 2½ hours. With this I serve Pot Roast, a delightful combo.

Use a 4 lb. cross rib pot roast. Do not use arm or anything off the rump. Brown in butter and olive oil or bacon dripping. Remove, deglaze pan with ½ c. of sweet Marsala wine. Add two jars of Boston Beef gravy. Add two ribs of celery cut in 4: length and a small onion, cut in quarters. Pour gravy and wine mixture over the meat and roast slowly (300 degrees) for three hours, turning over every ½ hour. Oops, I forgot to season the chicken and the roast with freshly ground pepper and Lawry's seasoned salt...deliscioso. Serves about six. This pot roast recipe goes well with moose or venison as well.

MEATBALLS BY TAMMI

My brother Mark's favorite

2 medium size raw potatoes	1 large carrot
1 tsp. salt	2 cans cream of chicken soup
2-3 onions	¼ tsp. pepper
1-2 eggs	2 lbs. ground beef

Grate potatoes, onions and carrots. Mix with two pounds of beef, eggs, salt and pepper. Make into round balls and place in casserole or large pan. Dilute 2 cans of soup with 1 can of milk or water. Bring to a boil. Pour over meatballs and bake in 350-degree oven for two hours.

SARMA BALLS

Sister-in-law Tammi Meittunen's recipe. She brought these to our Meittunen/Miettunen reunion this summer and they were a hit.

1 lb. each of ground beef, ground pork and ground ham
1 c. minute rice, uncooked
1 egg
1 clove garlic, chopped
½ c. water
1 onion, chopped
1 bag sauerkraut
1 can chicken broth
Butter

Mix first three ingredients and shape into meatballs; place in 9 x 13" pan. Sauté onion in butter, add garlic. Remove from heat and add sauerkraut, chicken broth and water. Pour mixture over meatballs and bake covered for 1-1/2 hours at 350 degrees.

SARMA'S

Recipe from Kevin Noonan of Keewatin.

½ head garlic
1 T. pepper
1½ large onions
5 eggs
3 lbs. ground beef
3 lbs. ground ham
2 c. rice (uncooked)
2 or 3 cabbage or sour heads
1 qt. sauerkraut

Mix garlic, pepper, onion and eggs in blender. Mix it with ham, beef and rice. Roll the mixture up in the cabbage or sour heads and place in roaster and cover with sauerkraut and tomato sauce. Add water in roaster almost to the top. Bake at 350 degrees for 2 or 3 hours.

VEAL OSCAR

I remember when we were living in Minneapolis; this was one of my favorites when going out on the town. I had forgotten about this tasty dish, perhaps because it is not served in Side Lake.

Chicken or turkey cutlets can be used (pound out breasts between waxed or parchment paper).
1 bunch asparagus spears, ends trimmed
1 pound king crab legs
Water
White wine
Lemon slices
½ c. flour
1 tsp. salt
½ tsp. black pepper
6 veal cutlets, lightly pounded
2 T. butter, divided
1 shallot, chopped
1 T. fresh tarragon, chopped
1 T. olive oil

Blanch asparagus tips in simmering water, drain and set aside. Poach crab legs in water, white wine and lemon slices for 5 minutes, then shell with a crab cracker and reserve.

In a shallow dish combine flour, salt and pepper; coat pieces of veal. In a sauté pan over medium heat, melt 1 tablespoon of butter and fry cutlets 3 minutes each side until golden brown. Remove the veal to a warm platter. Using the same pan, melt remaining butter. Stir in shallots and tarragon. Add olive oil, asparagus and crab. Sauté 2 minutes to warm.

To serve: place asparagus and crab on top of each cutlet. Drizzle each with Béarnaise Sauce, Serve hot.

Béarnaise Sauce:
¼ c. fresh tarragon, chopped
2 shallots, minced
¼ c. champagne vinegar
¼ c. dry white wine
3 egg yolks
1 stick butter, melted
Salt and pepper to taste

continued...

VEAL OSCAR continued...

In a small saucepan, combine the tarragon, shallots, vinegar and wine over medium-high heat. Bring to a simmer and cook until reduced by half. Remove from heat and set aside.

Place a stainless steel bowl in a saucepan containing simmering water, or use a double boiler. Whisk the egg yolks until doubled in volume.

Slowly add the melted butter; continue beating until sauce is thickened. Stir in reserved shallot reduction. Season with salt and pepper; set aside wrapped in a warm towel until time to serve over veal.

YOU ARE FROM THE IRON RANGE IF......
You think of the major food groups as
venison, walleye, and Schmidt.

You use a down comforter in the summer.

WHAT'S THE DIFFERENCE BETWEEN
A BOSS AND THE POPE?
The Pope only expects you to kiss his ring.

Chicken

CHICKEN PAPRIKA

1 chicken, 3-4 lbs.
1T. bacon or use butter
Salt to taste
½ c. sour cream

1 medium onion, chopped
½ tsp. paprika
1½ c. water
2 T. flour

Cut chicken into small pieces. Wilt onion in bacon or butter. Add paprika, chicken and salt, brown. Add water, cover and simmer until tender (about 45 minutes). Remove chicken from pan. Mix sour cream with flour, stir carefully into pan; simmer gravy for 5 minutes. Strain over chicken. Serves 4-5.

CHICKEN WITH BACON AND SCALLIONS

4 oz. bacon, thinly sliced
1½ lbs. boneless, skinless chicken breasts
Salt and pepper
3 scallions
2 T. white wine or chicken stock

Cut the bacon into ½" pieces. Cut the chicken, across the grain into ½" slices and toss with ¼ tsp. salt. Cut the scallions, including the green tops, into thin slices. Brown the bacon in a large frying pan. Remove it from the pan. Put chicken in the pan and sear over medium-high heat, stirring frequently, about 3 minutes. Add the cooked bacon and cook for about 5 minutes. Add wine and stir to deglaze. Stir in scallions. Serve with rice or buttered noodles.

CAJUN BOIL

From the Borovac Bunch
Warning: These crazed men put so much Cajun spices in it, most of us go hungry because we don't want our hair to fall out. I will give you their version and then you can cut way, way back! I have also cut the recipe in half. This will serve 8 to 10 people. Cook outside with large stainless steel pan over a gas tank.

2 whole chickens
4 Polish Kielbasa, cut in thirds
1 bag frozen shrimp
4 pounds red potatoes, whole (not peeled)
5 onions, quartered
5 c corn (cut in half)
4 packages whole mushrooms
4 whole garlic bulbs, paper removed
2 c. Cajun seasoning (Buy Cajun seasoning at grocery store.

continued...

CAJUN BOIL continued...
I would start with 1/2 cup and then add more as desired,)
Fill steel container about half full of water and add 2 cups of Cajun boil
seasoning (put in amount that you desire). Bring to a rolling boil. Add chickens;
cook 20 minutes. Add potatoes, sausage and garlic; cook 10 more minutes. Add
corn, mushrooms and onions; cook 10 more minutes. Add shrimp; cook for 5
minutes. DRAIN. Leftovers are great! Make sure the water is boiling throughout
the entire process.

This is more of a ritual,I think. We watch and take bets on which person sweats
the most while eating this wonderful "Cajun Boil". I normally bring a ham
sandwich!

CHICKEN CACCIATORE
An updated version adding oven-roasted tomatoes, mushrooms, and onions.

1½ pounds plum tomatoes, coarsely chopped (4 cups)
8 ounces crimini mushrooms
1 very large red onion, thinly sliced (about 3 cups)
5 T. olive oil, divided
2 T. Sherry wine vinegar
1-4½ to 4¾ pound chicken, cut into 8 pieces, excess fat trimmed
1½ T. chopped fresh rosemary, divided
½ c. dry red wine
1-14½ oz. can diced tomatoes in juice
1 c. low-salt chicken broth
1/3 c. thinly sliced basil, divided
2 T. drained capers, divided (optional)
12 ounces penne pasta, freshly cooked

Preheat oven to 400 degrees. Combine plum tomatoes, mushrooms, and onion in
large bowl. Add 3 T. oil and vinegar; toss to blend. Sprinkle generously with salt
and pepper. Spread vegetable mixture in single layer on large rimmed baking
sheet. Roast union onion slices are golden brown and all vegetables are tender,
stirring frequently, about 50 minutes. Remove from oven and set aside. Reduce
oven temperature to 350 degrees.

Sprinkle chicken with salt, pepper, and 1 T. rosemary. Heat remaining 2 T. oil in
heavy large deep ovenproof skillet over medium-high heat. Add wine to skillet and
boil to half, scraping up reduced wine browned bits. Add chicken and sauté until
golden brown, about 6 minutes per side. Transfer chicken to bowl.

continued...

CHICKEN CACCIATORE continued...

Add wine to skillet and boil until half, scraping up reduces wine browned bits, about 1 minute. Stir in canned tomatoes with juice, then broth and bring to boil. Reduce heat to medium and simmer 10 minutes to blend flavors. Return chicken to sauce in skillet. Place skillet in oven and roast uncovered until chicken is cooked through and juices run clear when pierced with knife, about 25 minutes. Remove skillet from oven. Stir in roasted vegetables, remaining ½ T. rosemary, half of basil, and half of capers. Simmer over medium heat until vegetables are heated through. Season with salt and pepper.

Place pasta in large shallow bowl. Top with chicken and sauce. Sprinkle remaining basil and capers over.

CHICKEN IN WINE SAUCE

Jerry Altman from Hibbing is one fine cook

2 cut up fryer chickens, cleaned, rinsed and patted dry
1 T. each olive and canola oil
5 cloves garlic, minced
2 c. chicken broth
1 T. dried rosemary leaves
1 large onion, diced
1½ c. dry white wine
2 T. Italian seasoning (dried)
Salt, pepper, parsley

Trim fat from chicken pieces; flavor with salt and pepper, and sauté slowly on medium heat, in olive oil and canola oil. When both sides are golden brown, (about 40 minutes) remove chicken from pan. Reserve two tablespoons oil and discard the rest. Meanwhile, chop the onion finely and mince the garlic cloves. Set aside.

Sauté Italian seasonings, rosemary, and garlic and onions. When onions are opaque (be careful not to burn the garlic), add wine and 1 cup of the chicken broth, scraping all the flavorings with a wooden spoon (deglazing).

Return chicken to pan and simmer down about 45 minutes or until chicken is tender and liquid is reduced, adding the other cup of chicken broth (or water) if needed while simmering. Serve on a large platter garnished with parsley and sauce. Pasta of your choice is excellent with strained liquid from the skillet pan as a side dish.

Chicken/Duck/Pheasant

ASIAN CHICKEN

1 T. oil
1 tsp. curry powder
Peanut Sauce

1 clove garlic, crushed
1 boneless, skinless chicken breast

Put a heavy skillet over medium heat. Add the oil, garlic, and curry powder, and stir for a few seconds to flavor the oil. Add the chicken breast, and sauté for about 7 minutes on each side, or until done through. Serve with the peanut sauce, warming it first.

Low-Cal Peanut Sauce:

1 piece of fresh ginger about the size of a walnut, peeled and thinly sliced across the grain
½ c. creamy peanut butter
½ c. chicken broth
1½ tsp. lemon juice
1½ tsp. soy sauce
¼ tsp. Tabasco sauce
1 large or 2 small cloves garlic, crushed
1½ tsp. Splenda

Put all the ingredients in a blender, and run it until everything is well combined and smooth. If you'd like it a little thinner, add another tablespoon of chicken broth. Yield: About 2 cups or 16 servings.

DUCK PICCATA

1/3 c. all-purpose flour
½ tsp. salt
¼ tsp. freshly ground pepper
2 boneless skinless whole wild duck breasts (8 to 12 oz. each) split in half, pounded to ¼" thickness
3 T. butter
¼ c. dry white wine
3 T. fresh lemon juice
2 T. capers, drained

In shallow dish, combine flour, salt and pepper. Dredge breast halves in flour mixture to coat. In 12" nonstick skillet, melt butter over medium heat. Add breast halves. Cook for 8 to 10 minutes, or until meat is browned, turning occasionally. Transfer breast halves to warm platter. Cover to keep warm. Set aside. To same skillet, add wine and juice. Stir to loosen browned bits in skillet. Cook for 3 to 5 minutes, or until sauce is reduced slightly. Remove from heat. Stir in capers. Spoon sauce over breast halves. Garnish with fresh lemon slices, if desired.

Duck/Pheasant

GRILLED DUCK

2 boneless skinless whole wild duck breasts (8 to 12 oz. each) split in half
1 medium red cooking apple, cored and cut into ¼" slices
1 medium onion, sliced
1 can (8 oz.) sliced water chestnuts, rinsed and drained
½ tsp. seasoned salt
¼ tsp. freshly ground pepper

Prepare grill for barbecuing. Place 1 breast half in center of 12 x 12" square of heavy-duty foil. Repeat with remaining breast halves. Arrange apple, onion and water chestnuts evenly over breast halves.

Sprinkle evenly with salt and pepper. Fold opposite sides of foil together in locked folds. Fold and crimp ends.

Place packets on cooking grate. Grill for 30 to 45 minutes, or until meat is tender and juices run clear.

Serves 4.

CREAMED PHEASANT OR PARTRIDGE

1/3 c. all-purpose flour
½ tsp. salt
½ tsp. pepper
¼ tsp. lemon pepper
¼ tsp. garlic powder
¼ tsp. paprika
1 dressed pheasant, cut up, skin removed
3 T. vegetable oil
1 c. whipping cream

Heat oven to 300 degrees.

In large plastic food-storage bag, combine flour, salt, peppers, garlic powder and paprika. Add pheasant pieces. Shake to coat.

In 10" nonstick skillet, heat oil over medium-high heat. Add pheasant pieces. Cook for 10 to 12 minutes, or until meat is browned, turning occasionally.

Place pheasant pieces in 2-qt. casserole. Pour cream over pieces. Bake for 1 to 1½ hours, or until meat is tender.

3 to 4 servings.

EASY SHRIMP SCAMPI

1 LB. 20-24 count shrimp
1 c. Newman's Italian dressing
1 T. butter
Juice of 1 lemon
½ c. white wine
2 cloves galic, chopped fine
Freshly ground black pepper

Peel and de-vein the shrimp. Marinate shrimp in Italian Dressing for ½ hour. Place shrimp in hot saute pan and cook until pink, turning halfway through cooking. Trnafer Shrimp to platter. Add butter, lemon juice and white wine to pan. Cook untill reduced by half. pour over shrimp and sprinkle with peeper. Serve immediately.

COCONUT SHRIMP

From a well-known restaurant

1½ lb. large raw shrimp
½ c. all-purpose flour
½ c. cornstarch
1 T. salt
½ T. white pepper
2 T. vegetable oil
1 c. ice water
Oil for deep frying
2 c. short shredded coconut
½ c. orange marmalade
¼ c. Gray Poupon country mustard
¼ c. honey
3-4 drops Tabasco sauce

Peel, devein and wash shrimp. Dry well on paper towels. Set aside. In a bowl, mix all dry ingredients for batter. Add 2T. oil and ice water. Stir to blend.

To fry: heat oil to 350 degrees in deep fryer or electric skillet. Spread coconut on a flat pan a little at a time, adding more as needed. Dip shrimp in batter, then roll in coconut. Fry in hot oil until lightly browned, about 4 minutes.

Bake at 300 degrees for 5 minutes to finish cooking of the shrimp. Serve with sweet and sour sauce or the following sauce: See above – combine marmalade, Grey Poupon mustard, honey and Tabasco sauce to taste.

SHRIMP WITH SPICY ORANGE FLAVOR

¼ c. extra-virgin olive oil
3 or 4 large cloves garlic, cut into thin slivers
2 or more small dried hot red chiles
Peel from 1 orange, grated
1 orange freshly squeezed
16 large shrimp, peeled
Salt, to taste
¼ c. minced cilantro leaves
1 T. freshly squeezed lemon juice, or to taste

Combine the oil and garlic in a skillet no larger than 10" across. Turn the heat to medium and cook until the garlic begins to sizzle, then turn the heat to medium-low. When the garlic is blond, stir in chiles, orange peel, and orange juice. Add the shrimp, and raise the heat to high. Cook, stirring occasionally and sprinkling with salt, until the shrimp are all pink, about 4 minutes. Remove from heat, and add most of the cilantro and the lemon juice. Taste, and adjust seasoning. Serve garnished with the remaining cilantro. Serves 4.

FRIED BLUEGILLS OR CRAPPIES

The secret of this recipe is the double dipping.
How I love to catch these fish and eat them!!

1 c. seasoned bread crumbs
1 c. grated Parmesan cheese (or use less)
½ tsp. salt
½ tsp. lemon-pepper seasoning
¼ tsp. pepper
6 eggs
1½ lbs. bluegills or crappies
½ c. vegetable oil, divided

In a shallow bowl, combine the first five ingredients. In another bowl, whisk the eggs. Dip fish in eggs, then coat with crumb mixture. Dip again in eggs and crumb mixture.

In a large skillet over medium-high heat, cook fish in batches in 2 tablespoons oil for 2-3 minutes on each side or until fish flakes easily with a fork, adding oil as needed. 6 servings.

Never, under any circumstances, take a sleeping pill and a laxative on the same night.

OVEN FRIED FISH FILLETS

4 T. (½ stick) unsalted butter
2/3 c. crushed crackers (preferably Ritz)
¼ c. grated Parmesan cheese
½ tsp. dried basil
½ tsp. dried oregano
¼ tsp. garlic powder
1 pound walleye, northerns (whatever)
Lemon wedges

Preheat oven to 350 degrees.
Melt the butter in a 9x13" pan in the oven. While it melts, combine everything else except the fish in a pie pan. Dip the fish around in the melted butter, dip each piece in the crumb mixture, and return it to the baking pan.

Bake the fillets for 20 to 25 minutes, or until the fish flakes with a fork. Serve with lemon wedges. Serves 4.

SPICY FRIED FISH

Vegetable oil
1-1/4 c. cornmeal
1 tsp. salt
½ tsp. ground red pepper (cayenne) or to your taste
¼ tsp. pepper
6 small fish (about ½ pound each) skinned and cleaned
½ c. all-purpose flour
2 eggs, slightly beaten

Heat oven to 275 degrees. Heat oil (½ ") in 12" skillet over medium-high heat until hot.

Mix cornmeal, salt, red pepper, and pepper; reserve. Coat fish with flour; dip into eggs. Coat with cornmeal mixture. Fry fish two at a time until golden brown, about 6 minutes on each side. Keep warm in oven while frying remaining fish. Garnish with lemon wedges if desired.

"Old is when......Your friends compliment you on your new alligator shoes and you are barefoot."

"Old is when.......getting lucky means you find your car in the parking lot."

PAN FISH

Allow ½ pound of fish per person
Rinse and drain fish; pat dry with paper towels. Broil in well greased shallow pan or well greased grill over medium-hot coals.

Combine ½ c. vegetable oil, ¼ c. lemon juice, 2 tsp. salt, ½ tsp. Worcestershire sauce, ¼ tsp. pepper and dash Tabasco sauce; brush on fish. Cook 4" from heat 5 to 7 minutes. Baste and turn. Cook until fish flakes easily with fork, 3 to 5 minutes.

SALMON DICK NOBLE

Dick Noble formerly of the fish farm in Chisholm now lives in Washington.

Fillet(s) of salmon or large trout – enough for about ½ lb. per person.

Place fillet(s) skin side down on foil with ends and sides of the foil pinched up to form a pan. Add salt, pepper, lemon pepper, garlic and parsley flakes and allow to marinate in the refrigerator for a few hours. Even overnight does not create a problem. When ready for the b-b-q, melt butter with added garlic and a bit of lemon juice and spread over each fillet. Use some dry alder ships for a smoke flavor.

Spread the butter/garlic paste over the fish after about 10 minutes in the b-b-q. Test to see if cooked through at about 20 minutes. Normally the fish will be done in 20 to 30 minutes depending on thickness of the fish. You can broil in an oven if desired, but don't add the alder chips.

ITALIAN FISH

Joe Iozzo,Jr. – our favorite on Friday's during lent.

1 lb. fish (pollock, cod, walleye)
¼ c. olive oil
2 sliced onions
1 jar Prego Chunky Garden spaghetti sauce
1 lb. angel hair pasta

Lightly sauté onions in oil and season to taste. Spread onions about 1" deep in baking pan and lay seasoned fish on top (use any of your favorite seasonings). Bake at 350 degrees for about 25 minutes.

Flip onions and fish upside down on serving platter and top with heated spaghetti sauce. Serve over pasta.

NORTHERN CRAB CAKES

Here is sister Carole and husband Mike Borovac's perfected recipe for "crab cakes" using northerns. Carole said he is "coo coo" over this recipe. Of course, I knew he was "coo coo" long ago.

Poach one pound of northern (skin off) in boiling water with a tablespoon of white vinegar for 3 or 4 minutes. Cool in colander and take out bones.

Combine:
Cooled northern (in flakes like crab)
¼ c. diced green onion
¼ c. red pepper, diced
½ c. seasoned Italian bread crumbs
½ c. mayonnaise
¼ c. cream cheese, softened
1 T. Dijon mustard
1 egg, beaten
½ tsp. tarragon, optional
1/8
 tsp. cayenne pepper
¼ tsp. salt
2 T. vegetable oil for frying

Combine all and flatten in patties. Roll in about 2½ cups of seasoned Italian bread crumbs. Refrigerate for at least ½ hour or overnight. Don't make them very big or they will break.

Fry in hot oil until golden brown on both sides.

Makes 24 appetizers or 6 entrée cakes.

REMEDY FOR GOUT
**Canned red cherries packed in water. Usually takes 2 cans.
Divide each can into thirds and eat them 3 times a day.**

TURKEY DRESSING

Some people call it stuffing – whatever. Yes, there is a pound of butter in the dressing.

Take enough of yesterday's bread (unsliced, if possible) and cut off the outside crust. Cut the trimmed loaf into hunks just big enough to make a good handful. With a fairly coarse grater, crumble the bread into a big dishpan. This will give you a panful of nice fluffy grated bread. It will take about three small loaves for a 15 to 18 pound turkey.

Chop a medium onion into fine particles. One onion is plenty. Stir in onion evenly into bread, add the powdered sage (to taste), shaking it lightly as you stir it into the bread and not too much sage, just enough to taste tangy.

Melt one pound of butter and pour the melted butter slowly over the mass while you stir it in evenly.

TURKEY LO-FAT SAUSAGE
Marge Ranta Radel

1 lb. ground turkey
1 clove garlic (or ½ tsp. garlic powder)
½ tsp. fennel seed
¼ c. wine
1 tsp. parsley
Hot pepper flakes
Salt and pepper to taste

Mix and let stand 1 hour to blend.

Eagles may soar, but weasels don't get sucked into jet engines.

TURKEY OR CHICKEN HOT DISH
8 slices of cooked turkey or chicken
1 onion, chopped
1 c. mushroom pieces
½ tsp. salt
1 T. paprika
Dash nutmeg
Heavy cream
Grated parmesan cheese

Cook onions and mushrooms in butter for five minutes.

Combine with seasonings and spread in bottom of baking dish. Lay chicken or turkey slices on top. Add cream to cover. Sprinkle with cheese.

Bake at 400 degrees until bubbly.

TURKEY STUFFING
4 eggs
½ c. bread crumbs
½ c. chopped celery
½ envelope Lipton onion soup
1 c. uncooked popcorn

Beat eggs and add other ingredients.

Stuff a 16 to 20 pound turkey.

Bake at 375 degrees oven for 3 hours or until the ass blows off the turkey.

When Hibbing was moved in 1916, each building was jacked up, wheels were put underneath, and they were towed away, one at a time. It took 1-1/2 years to get everything moved.
The Mes-Ver Iron Range, p.6.

TURKEY PIE

Use your left over turkey and dressing. This is very good!

Pastry:
1½ c. sifted flour
1½ tsp. baking powder
¼ tsp. salt
½ c. shortening
3/8 c. hot water
1 T. lemon juice
1 egg yolk, unbeaten
1 whole egg

Filling:
1¾ c. left over bread dressing (stuffing)
3 c. cooked turkey
1-4 oz. can mushrooms
2 c. gravy
1 T. butter

English pastry:
Resift flour with baking powder and salt. Mix well and stir into flour mixture: shortening, hot water, lemon juice and unbeaten egg yolk. Chill.

While pastry is being chilled prepare the ingredients for the filling.

Remove roast turkey from the bones and cut into pieces enough to make three cups.

Drain the mushrooms saving the liquid. Sauté mushrooms in 1T. butter. Heat the gravy and mushroom liquid . Gravy may be extended with medium white sauce.

Roll out ¾ of the chilled pastry on very lightly floured board and line a 1½ quart casserole. Fill with alternate layers of cold stuffing, pieces of turkey, sautéed mushrooms and gravy in this order.

Roll out remaining pastry and place over filling, sealing edges and making slits in top.

Brush with slightly beaten egg and bake at 425 degrees for 35 minutes. Serve hot.

SPAM KABOBS

My friend Tom Sersha loves Spam – this one is for you!

Skewer Spam chunks, pineapple chunks, sweet pickle slices. Brush with Italian dressing and grill, basting occasionally.

SPAM AND RICE HOT DISH

Spam is kind of a cult thing and is coming back. As a newlywed, I would slice Spam, put a little brown sugar on each slice and stick it with cloves and fry in the pan. I really thought I was cookin'.

Sauté in butter:
1 green pepper, chopped
1 c. celery, chopped
1 onion, chopped

1 can Spam, cut into small squared
1 can mushroom soup
1 c. water
1 c. rice, parboiled until about half done
1 can chow mein noodles

Add the Spam to browned onion and celery mixture. Then add the soup and water mix. In a 9x13" pan or casserole dish, put chow mein noodles, then rice, then cover with the soup mixture. Bake for 45 minutes at 350 degrees.

JOE'S VENISON DINNER

Joe Stukel – see his picture and story in back of book.

Use a 4 quart pressure cooker

Brown venison steaks or chops in a frying pan.
Add salt, pepper and ¼ c. chopped garlic. Place in the pressure cooker.

Saute in frying pan:
2 c. chopped onion   2 c. chopped celery
1 c. shredded carrots   1 c. chopped green pepper
Two strip of cut bacon

Put all in pressure cooker. In the cooker add 5 or 6 medium pierced potatoes and carrots. Add 1 can of beef broth. Cook for 30 minutes on #10 setting, after jiggle (What is a jiggle?)

VENISON SALAMI
4 lbs. ground venison
2 c. cold water
3 tsp. liquid smoke
½ tsp. black pepper
½ tsp. garlic powder
½ tsp. onion powder
2 tsp. mustard seed
6 T. Morton's Tender Quick

In a large bowl, mix all ingredients together and knead well. Divide into four rolls and wrap in foil, shiny side in. Punch holes in the bottom of the rolls. Refrigerate for 24 hours. Bake on broiler rack at 350 degrees for 1½ hours.

BEEF OR VENISON JERKY
My sister-in-law Ruth Meittunen makes this for my brother Roger.

2 lbs. lean beef (family steak) or venison.
Partially defrost and cut into slices diagonally.

Mix together:
2 tsp. liquid smoke
2/3 tsp. garlic powder
1/3 tsp. pepper
2 tsp. onion salt
2 tsp. accent
½ c. Worcestershire sauce
½ c. soy sauce

Put about 2 tsp. of sauce to cover bottom of glass cake pan. Add a layer of meat. Repeat until meat is all covered. Top with foil and refrigerate 8 hours to marinate.

Pat each slice of meat with paper towel to get out excess sauce. Line meat on racks in oven.

Set oven temperature for lowest heat and bake 15 to 20 minutes. Shut off oven for 3 hours. Put oven on again (leaving oven door ajar) for 10 to 15 minutes. Turn off oven and let set again for 3 hours.

Test for dryness. If thicker slices are not dry, repeat above.

Cool, store loosely in covered jar.

Photo taken in 1938 of
Dad with his 1936 Ford

Brother Roger with His 1938 Ford

THE CENTERFOLD

JOE IOZZO, JR.
MY NEIGHBOR FROM HELL

VENISON AND SAUERKRAUT WITH NOODLES
Donald Schnortz III makes this delicious dish.

2 T. vegetable oil
1½ lbs. venison stew meat, cut into 1" cubes
1 can (16 oz.) Bavarian-style sauerkraut
2 c. water
1 small onion, sliced
1 pkg. (1.75 oz.) beefy mushroom soup mix
2 T. packed brown sugar
2 T. red wine vinegar
1 tsp. soy sauce
½ tsp. ground ginger
Hot buttered noodles

Heat oven to 350 degrees. In 6-qt. ovenproof Dutch oven or stockpot, heat oil over medium-high heat. Add venison cubes. Cook for 3 to 5 minutes, or just until meat is browned, stirring frequently. Add remaining ingredients, except noodles. Mix well. Cover. Bake for 1 to 1-1/2 hours, or until meat is tender, stirring occasionally. Serve mixture over noodles. Garnish with snipped fresh parsley, if desired. Serves 4 to 6.

LEMON-GARLIC VENISON TENDERLOIN
2 tsp. snipped fresh parsley
1 clove garlic, minced
½ tsp. grated lemon peel
½ tsp. freshly cracked peppercorns
1 T. olive oil
1/8 tsp. salt
1 venison tenderloin (8 oz.) cut in half crosswise

In small mixing bowl, combine parsley, garlic, peel and pepper. Rub steaks evenly on both sides with parsley mixture. Let stand at room temperature for 15 minutes. In 10" nonstick skillet, heat oil over medium heat. Sprinkle salt over oil. Add steaks. Cook for 6 to 8 minutes, or until meat is desired doneness, turning steaks over once.

VENISON MEATLOAF
1/3 c. catsup
2 T. barbecue sauce
2 T. French dressing

Meatloaf:
2 lbs. lean ground venison
1 c. canned piccalilli* or pickled mixed garden vegetables, rinsed and drained
½ c. chopped onion
½ c. coarsely crushed seasoned croutons
2 eggs, beaten
½ tsp. seasoned salt

Heat oven to 350 degrees.

In small mixing bowl, combine catsup, barbecue sauce and dressing. Set aside. In large mixing bowl, combine 3T. catsup mixture and the meatloaf ingredients.

Spray 9 x 5" loaf dish with nonstick vegetable cooking spray.   Press meatloaf mixture into prepared dish. Spoon remaining catsup mixture evenly over meatloaf.

Bake for 1 to 1-1/2 hours, or until meat is firm and no longer pink. Let stand for 10 minutes before slicing. Serves 8.

*Piccalilli recipe on page 120 of "To Mom With Love".

VENISON CHILI
The acid in the wine and vinegar tenderizes the venison. It will be well worth your effort.

4 T. butter	1 red onion, chopped
4 cloves garlic, minced	4 T. dark brown sugar
3 c. red wine	4 T. red wine vinegar
4 T. tomato paste	4 c. chicken broth
1 tsp. ground cumin	½ tsp. cayenne pepper
½ tsp. chili powder	2 T. chopped fresh cilantro
4 T. canola oil	10 slices cooked bacon, diced

2 pounds venison stew meat, trimmed and finely diced
2 c. black beans, cooked and drained
Salt to taste

continued...

VENISON CHILI continued...

In a large pot, sauté the onion and garlic in the butter over medium-high heat for 3 to 4 minutes.

Stir in the brown sugar and continue to cook for 2 to 3 minutes.

Stir in the red wine, vinegar, tomato paste, chicken broth, cilantro and spices.

Simmer uncovered for 30 to 35 minutes, or until the mixture is reduced by about half.

Meanwhile, heat the oil in a large skillet; stir in the bacon and fry for 3 to 4 minutes or until browned. Move the bacon to one side of the skillet and add the venison to the empty side.

Season the meat with salt to taste and sauté for 15 minutes, or until well browned.

Stir in the beans and toss all together. Transfer this mixture to the simmering pot, mix thoroughly and simmer for about 20 minutes, or until tender.

Yield: 8 servings.

SLOW-COOKED VENISON ROAST

3 pounds boneless venison roast
1 large onion, sliced
1 T. soy sauce
1 T. Worcestershire sauce
1 T. garlic salt
¼ tsp. ground black pepper
1 (1 oz.) package dry onion soup mix
1 (10.75 oz.) can condensed cream of mushroom soup

Put cleaned meat in slow cooker and cover with onion. Sprinkle with soy sauce, Worcestershire sauce, garlic salt and pepper. In a small bowl, combine the soup mix and the soup and pour mixture over venison.

Cook on low for 6 hours.

Yield: 6 to 8 servings.

Marinades/Salsa/Sauces

Uncle Lester Williams,
Hibbing Graduating Class of 1936
story on page 164

MARINADES

Ginger root is one of the best ways to tenderize meat. Also vinegar, citrus and wine will do the trick. Because marinades contain acid ingredients, the marinating should be done in a glass, ceramic or stainless-steel container. Don't marinate in aluminum.

TERIYAKI MARINADE
¼ c. oil
¼ c. soy sauce
2 T. ketchup
1 T. lemon juice
1 T. vinegar
¼ tsp. pepper
1 T. sliced fresh ginger
1 tsp. garlic powder

Mix well, pour into a large zip-type plastic bag and add to venison or beef and seal. Turn several times to make sure all of the meat is covered, then allow to marinate in the refrigerator for 8 to 12 hours ahead of cooking, turning a couple of times. The tougher the meat, the longer you should marinate. Venison can marinate up to four days if quite tough. This recipe will handle approximately six steaks.

LIME OR LEMON MARINADE
½ c. olive oil
1/3 c. chopped oregano
1 c. lime or lemon juice
1 tsp. ground cumin
2 T. minced garlic

Great for fish also.

MARINADE FOR STEAKS
Coke-Cola
2 T. soy sauce
1 tsp. garlic powder.

SOUTHERN MEAT MARINADE
2 qts. apple juice
1 c. Worcestershire sauce
1 c. orange juice
1 c. light brown sugar
½ c. olive oil
½ c. lemon juice
2 T. hot sauce
½ c. apple cider vinegar
½ c. salt

Heat and whisk together until sugar and salt dissolve.

MARINADE FOR SHRIMP
1 T. grated orange peel
½ c. orange juice
2 T. olive oil
½ tsp. salt
½ tsp. crushed red pepper
2 cloves garlic, crushed
16 shrimp

Combine ingredients and marinade shrimp and then grill.

Tips:

Perfect meatballs....When you are making a large batch of meatballs, shape the mixture into a log and cut off slices. The slices roll easily into balls.

Rinse bacon under cold water before frying. This reduces the amount bacon shrinks by about 50%. Try it!!

When making beef stew using a cheaper cut of beef, add sweet-pickle juice. The vinegar tenderizes the meat and adds great flavor!

To cut onions without tears, cut them either under cold water or wet the knife several times while using.

GREAT PEANUT SAUCE
This is a good sauce to pour over vegetables or as a dipping sauce for chicken.

1 c. peanut butter
1 c. hot water
½ c. white vinegar
¼ c. soy sauce
¼ c. molasses
1 tsp. cayenne pepper (or less)

In a small saucepan, whisk together peanut butter and water over low heat. Stir in vinegar, soy sauce, molasses and cayenne pepper. Heat through, but do not simmer or boil; cooking may cause the sauce to curdle. Yield: 3 cups.

CHEESE SAUCE
2 T. butter or margarine
2 T. all-purpose flour
1 tsp. salt
1 c. milk
1 c. shredded cheddar cheese
1 tsp. prepared mustard
½ tsp. Worcestershire sauce
Salt and pepper, to taste

In a medium-size saucepan, melt butter. Mix in flour and 1 tsp. of salt. Stir continually until the mixture is simmering. Slowly pour milk into the mixture. Continue stirring over medium heat until the mixture has thickened. Stir in cheese, mustard and Worcestershire sauce. Continue stirring until all of the cheese is melted and the dip is smooth. Using pre-grated may produce a grainy texture as a result of the anti-caking ingredients found in pre-grated cheese.

Serve sauce over baked potatoes, vegetables or pasta, or as a dipping sauce.

Yield: 2 cups.

SAUCE FOR BEEF SANDWICHES
½ c. whipping cream (whipped)
2 T. creamy horseradish
1 tsp. lemon juice
Pinch of sugar

Beat cream first and then add rest of ingredients. Chill for 2 hours.

CHARLIE'S BAR-B-Q SAUCE
1 (18 oz.) bottle barbecue sauce
1 oz. Scotch whisky
1½ tsp. Worcestershire sauce
1½ T. white sugar
¼ tsp. hot pepper sauce
½ tsp. ground ginger
1/4 tsp. cayenne pepper
½ tsp. paprika
½ tsp. chili powder
½ tsp. garlic powder
½ tsp. onion powder
½ tsp. dried oregano
1T. red pepper flakes
½ tsp. ground black pepper

Mix all ingredients together in a small bowl. Cover and keep refrigerated until ready to use.

Yield: 2½ cups.

TARTAR SAUCE
2 T. tarragon vinegar
1 tsp. Dijon mustard
½ tsp. course salt
Pinch cayenne pepper
1/3 c. finely chopped pickles (I use sweet)
1 T. finely chopped shallots
1 tsp. finely chopped capers (optional)
1 T. finely chopped flat-leaf parsley
1 c. mayonnaise

In a medium bowl, combine the ingredients, and refrigerate. Makes 1½ cups.

ORANGE SHALLOT MAYONNAISE

Use this as a spread on roast pork or turkey sandwiches, or as a dip for grilled shrimp or as a dressing for a fruit salad.

1 to 2 oranges
3 T. finely chopped shallot
2/3 c. mayonnaise
½ tsp. fresh lemon juice
1/8 tsp. black pepper

TOMATO AND BASIL TOPPING

Spread this topping on bruschetta and serve immediately. Makes 2 cups.

3 beefsteak tomatoes, seeded and cut into ½" cubes
¼ tsp. salt
1/3 c. pitted and chopped black olives
2 T. chopped fresh basil
2 T. extra-virgin olive oil
1 garlic clove, crushed through a press
¼ tsp. crushed hot red pepper

Toss tomato cubes and salt in a colander. Let stand in a sink to drain off excess juices, about 30 minutes. Mix cubes, olives, basil, oil, garlic and red pepper in a medium bowl. Spread on brushetta.

ORANGE SALSA

½ c. fresh orange segments, diced
1 c. Roma tomatoes, diced
1 T. red onions, diced
1 tsp. jalapeno, minced
2 T. cilantro leaves, minced
1/8 tsp. salt

Combine diced orange segments, tomatoes, red onions, jalapeno, cilantro and salt. Toss gently to mix thoroughly. Cover and refrigerate until ready to serve.

TOMATO CORN SALSA
Great served on broiled hamburgers or turkey burgers.

12 cherry tomatoes, finely chopped
½ tsp. kosher salt
½ c. cooked fresh corn or thawed frozen corn kernels
1 T. fresh lime juice
1 garlic clove, minced
1 T. chopped fresh cilantro
2 tsp. olive oil
Additional kosher salt and ground black pepper to taste

Toss the tomatoes with the salt and drain in a colander for 15 minutes.

Combine the tomatoes and the rest of the ingredients, add salt, pepper and toss well.

STRAWBERRY SALSA
½ medium red onion, thinly sliced
1 jalapeno pepper, minced
½ red bell pepper, stemmed, seeded and julienned
½ green bell pepper, stemmed, seeded and julienned
¼ c. finely chopped fresh cilantro
1 c. fresh strawberries, hulled and sliced
¼ c. fresh orange juice
2 T. extra virgin olive oil
Salt and pepper, to taste

Place all ingredients in a large mixing bowl and toss to combine. Cover and refrigerate at least two hours or up to 4 hours. Fifteen minutes before serving, remove the salsa from the refrigerator so it loses some of its chill. This salsa can be served with tortilla chips.

Vegetables/Potatoes

William Meittunen
Graduate 1933 Hibbing High School
Swimming; Hi-Y; Reporter.
Brusque…ducky- he swims…
Thankful the government doesn't tax words.

CORN PUDDING

2 (14.75 oz.) cans cream-style corn
1 (11 oz.) can whole kernel corn, drained
4 eggs, well beaten
1/3 c. sugar
3 T. cornstarch
1 T. minced onions
1-1/2 tsp. Seasoned Salt
½ tsp. ground mustard
½ c. milk
¼ c. butter or margarine, melted

Preheat oven to 350 degree. Combine cream-style corn, whole kernel corn and eggs in large bowl. Add mixture of sugar, cornstarch, minced onion, seasoned salt and ground mustard. Stir in milk and melted butter. Pour mixture into greased 3-quart casserole dish. Bake 1 hour, stirring once.

Makes 12 servings.

SWEET POTATOES IN ORANGE CUPS

6 sweet potatoes, unpeeled
½ stick butter, softened
¼ c. orange juice
¼ c. chopped pecans
6 large oranges
48 mini-marshmallows

Preheat oven to 375 degrees. Cover sweet potatoes with cold water in a pot and boil until fork tender. Peel the potatoes; transfer to a bowl, and mash. Stir in butter, orange juice, and pecans and mix well. For the orange shells, cut each orange in half and scoop out the pulp using a small knife or grapefruit spoon. Reserve the pulp for another use. Fill each orange shell with the potato mixture and top off with the marshmallows. Bake until hot and the marshmallows are melted.

SWEET POTATO BALLS

Mash sweet potatoes. Form into balls. Put marshmallow inside. Roll in corn flakes.

Brown in hot oven, 10 minutes or so.

LUPINI BEANS
The Italians make this at Christmas

Put 2 pounds of Lupini beans to soak in a pan of water for one or two days. Then boil the beans for two hours. Continue soaking beans until they lose their bitterness, about 5 to 7 days. Change water every day or else keep a slow stream of water running through them. Serve with salt, pepper and oregano. Beans may be kept in refrigerator in water at least two weeks.

FRENCH BEAN SALAD
1 can corn (Mexican, for color)   1 can peas or peas with onions
1 can French style green beans   1 small jar pimentos

Drain well. Cut up and add: several stalks of celery, 1 medium onion and ½ to 1 green pepper. Mix all of above ingredients lightly with fork, adding salt to taste. Combine the following and pour over vegetables:

1 c. oil   ½ tsp. celery seed
1 c. vinegar   ½ tsp. mustard seed
1-1/2 c. sugar   ½ tsp. paprika

Refrigerate for 24 hours, drain before serving.

GREEN BEANS WITH ONIONS
1 T. olive oil
1 T. butter
1 small onion, chopped
2 tsp. minced garlic
Dash of seasoned salt or Greek seasoning
Black pepper, to taste
1 c. chicken broth
1 to 1-1/4 pounds trimmed green beans
Salt
Whole tomato, cut up

In a medium pan over medium heat add oil, butter and onion. Sauté onion 3 minutes add rest of ingredients. Add beans and cover pan and simmer 8 minutes or until tender.

4 Servings.

ITALIAN GREEN BEANS BY THE IOZZO'S

If you don't like vegetables, try these! Yum!

1 gallon bag of fresh green beans, snapped and washed.

Drizzle 1½ tsp. of olive oil in bottom of pan – add beans.

Slice one medium onion in rings, add to beans.

Cut one whole tomato in eight pieces and add to beans.

Add 2 tsp. minced garlic, seasoned salt, Greek seasoning to taste, and black pepper.

When onions look clear, squirt about a tsp. of catsup into beans.

Stir, cover, and cook about 30 minutes.

__Shunumitism__ – the belief that proximity to young person rejuvenates elders.

"If you consider it a sport to gather your food by drilling through 18" of ice and sitting there all day hoping that the food will swim by, "you might live in Minnesota." – __Jeff Foxworthy__

Remember "I" before "E", except for Budweiser.

BEANS WITH LIME BUTTER

½ lb. each fresh green and wax beans, trimmed
2 T. butter or margarine
2 tsp. snipped fresh dill
2 tsp. lime juice
1 tsp. grated lime peel
½ tsp. salt
¼ tsp. pepper

Place beans in a saucepan and cover with water; bring to a boil. Cook, uncovered, for 10 minutes or until crisp-tender; drain.

Melt butter in a skillet; add the dill, lime juice and peel, salt, pepper, and beans.

Stir to coat and cook until heated through.

4 servings.

MUSHROOMS AND ONIONS IN SOUR CREAM

This is a very rich and tasty side dish – yum!

1 large onion
2 cloves garlic, minced
1 lb. mushrooms
Salt and pepper
2 T. flour
½ c. heavy whipping cream
½ c. sour cream
Grated cheese (your choice)
Butter

Chop onion and garlic and sauté in ¼ c. butter.

Cut mushrooms into pieces. Add to onion and garlic, season and cook until liquid disappears.

Add flour and blend well. Add cream and sour cream and stir well.

Pour into greased baking dish, sprinkle with grated cheese, pour melted butter over top.

Place dish in shallow pan filled with water and bake in 350 degree oven for 30 minutes or until mixture becomes solid.

MRS. KILBOURNE'S LIMA BEAN CASSEROLE

My wonderful neighbor in St. Louis Park. I think she was in her 80's in 1965. She was related to Mary Todd Lincoln and had the napkin rings from his inauguration.

1 bag lima beans, soaked in water overnight
1 c. brown sugar
6 slices bacon, cut in pieces

Simmer beans with water (water to cover) about 45 minutes. Add sugar and bacon. Bake at 325 degrees for 1-1/2 hours.

Potatoes

POTATOES WHIPPED WITH CHEESE

From a restaurant in Aspen

3 lb. potatoes (cooked and whipped)
¼ lb. butter
6 oz. cream cheese
1 green pepper (chopped)
1 bunch scallions (sliced)
1 small can pimiento (with juice)
½ c. cheddar cheese (grated)
½ c. parmesan cheese (grated)
¼ tsp. saffron
Cream (optional)

Lightly salt the potatoes and blend in the above eight ingredients, beating constantly. The mixture should be fairly moist. If not, add a bit of cream and more butter. Pile into an ovenproof serving dish and bake uncovered at 350 degrees for 30 minutes. Serves 4-6.

This can be prepared well in advance of serving and popped into the oven when needed.

ZESTY MASHED POTATOES

5 c. freshly mashed potatoes
3 c. cream style cottage cheese
1 c. sour cream
2 T. grated onion
2-1/2 tsp. salt
¼ tsp. pepper
Melted butter
½ c. toasted almonds

continued.....

ZESTY MASHED POTATOES continued...

Mash potatoes thoroughly using no milk or butter. Buzz cottage cheese in a blender and mix into potatoes. Add all ingredients except butter and almonds. Spoon into 2-quart casserole. Brush surface with melted butter. Bake at 350 degrees for 30 minutes. Place under broiler for a few minutes to brown lightly. Sprinkle with almonds.

POTATOES GRATIN

2 lbs. white potatoes, peeled, sliced 1/8" thick
½ lb. grated Swiss cheese (or more)
Salt
Pepper
Dots of sweet butter
2 whole eggs
1-1/2 c. half-and-half

Place potato slices in cold water; drain, dry slices thoroughly with towel. Layer the potatoes in 2-quart casserole with lots of Swiss cheese, salt and freshly group pepper to taste. Top with additional cheese and dot with butter. Beat eggs with half-and-half. Pour over the potatoes and bake at 350 degrees for 1 hour and 15 minutes.

PARTY POTATOES

8 to 9 cups diced peeled potatoes
2 T. butter
2 T. milk
¾ tsp. salt
¼ tsp. pepper
1 pkg. (oz.) cream cheese, softened
1 carton (8 oz.) French onion dip
Paprika

In a large saucepan, cook potatoes in boiling salted water until tender, drain. Mash the potatoes with butter, milk, salt and pepper until smooth. Add cream cheese and onion dip; mix well. Spread in a greased 1-1/2 qt. baking dish. Sprinkle with paprika. Cover and refrigerated for 8 hours or overnight. Remove from the refrigerator 30 minutes before baking. Bake, uncovered, at 350 degrees for 50-60 minutes.

12-14 servings.

STUFFED CRAB PEPPERS

Kevin Noonan from Keewatin gave me this recipe. It was his grandmother's.

3 large green peppers
1 (8 oz.) can crabmeat
2 c. grated Cheddar cheese
1 c. cooked barley
1 can extra small peas
2 tsp. lemon juice
¼ tsp. Worcestershire sauce
Salt and pepper
2 T. butter
6 T. bread crumbs

Mix together the crabmeat, cheese, barley, peas, lemon juice, Worcestershire sauce, salt and pepper. Cut green peppers in half lengthwise and clean them out and fill with crab mixture. Cover the top of pepper with the butter and breadcrumbs. Bake at 350 degrees for 1 hour. Cover for 45 minutes. Uncover for 15 minutes or until golden brown.

STUFFED VIDALIA ONIONS

4 large Vidalia onions, peeled*
1 pkg. (10 oz.) frozen green peas
4 oz. fresh mushrooms, sliced
¼ tsp. dried thyme
1/8 tsp. pepper
2 T. butter or margarine
½ tsp. instant chicken bouillon granules
¼ c. hot water
*Substitute any large sweet onions if Vidalias are not available.

Slice tops off onions; hollow out center of each, leaving ¼" thick shell. Place shells in an 8" square baking dish. Combine peas, mushrooms, thyme and pepper; divide among shells. Dot each with ½ tablespoon butter. Dissolve bouillon in water; pour over onions. Cover dish with plastic wrap, turning back one edge to vent steam. Microwave on high 7 to 10 minutes or until tender, rotating onions halfway through cooking time. Baste with cooking liquid. Let stand, covered 3 minutes before serving.

Yield: 4 servings.

ZUCCHINI AND CORN CASSEROLE

2 medium zucchini, thinly sliced
1 medium green pepper, thinly sliced
1 medium sweet red pepper, thinly sliced
2 to 3 T. vegetable oil
2 c. fresh or frozen corn
1 tsp. garlic salt
½ tsp. Italian seasoning (or more to taste)

In a large skillet, sauté zucchini and peppers in oil until crisp-tender, about 4 minutes. Add remaining ingredients; sauté 3 to 4 minutes longer or until the corn is tender.

Yield: 10 servings.

GRILLED CORN ON THE COB

12 medium ears sweet corn
½ c. butter, softened
¼ c. sugar
1 c. minced fresh cilantro or parsley
Salt and pepper to taste

Soak corn in cold water for 1 hour. Drain and pat dry. In a small mixing bowl, beat the butter and sugar; spread over corn. On a shallow plate, combine the cilantro, salt and pepper. Roll corn in mixture until lightly coated. Wrap each ear in heavy-duty foil. Grill, covered, over medium heat for 25-30 minutes or until the corn is tender, turning occasionally.

SPAGHETTI SQUASH WITH GARLIC

Preheat oven to 400 degrees. With a fork, prick 2 spaghetti squash (2 pounds each) in several places. Place on a rimmed baking sheet; bake until soft to the touch, about 1 hour. When cool enough to handle, halve squash crosswise. Scoop out seeds; discard. Scrape flesh into strands.

In a large skillet, heat 2 T. olive oil over low heat. Add 2 slivered garlic cloves; cook until fragrant and just starting to color, about 5 minutes. Add squash; season with coarse salt and ground pepper. Cook, tossing frequently until squash is very hot, about 5 minutes.

Soups

Steve Kerzie Story on page 160

BEEF MOJAKKA
Aune Ruskanen made this recipe for husband Bill.

2 lb. stew meat
1 stalk celery, chopped
8 carrots, chopped
8 medium potatoes, diced
1 medium-large onion, diced
1 large rutabaga, diced
½ c. beef bouillon
1 head cabbage, chopped

Brown meat. Add water to cover and simmer about 30 minutes. Add celery and carrots; add water to cover ingredients and simmer about 30 minutes more. Add potatoes, onion, rutabaga, beef bouillon and enough water to cover ingredients. Simmer until vegetables are tender; add cabbage and simmer 10 minutes more.

CHEDDAR POTATO SOUP
2 packages (11.5 oz. each) Stouffer's frozen potatoes au gratin
2 c. whole milk
¼ c. Cheez Whiz
¾ c. shredded sharp cheddar cheese
½ c. green onions, chopped

Prepare potatoes in microwave according to package instructions. Whisk milk and Cheez Whiz in a heavy large saucepan to blend. Gently stir in potatoes. Bring mixture to a simmer over medium heat. Ladle soup equally into 4 bowls. Sprinkle generously with shredded cheese and green onions. Serve hot.

Makes 4 servings.

CHILI BEAN SOUP
1 lb. ground beef
1 (24 oz.) can V-8 juice
1 (8 oz.) can string beans including juice
A little onion or onion flakes
½ (or less) pkg. chili seasoning mix
A little salt

Fry meat; add other ingredients and simmer for a while. Serve with French or other crusty bread and a salad.

CHEESEBURGER SOUP

1 pound lean ground beef or ground venison
½ c. shredded carrots
½ c. chopped celery
½ c. chopped onion
3 c. chicken broth
2 c. cooked white rice
1 (15-oz) can mixed vegetables, drained
1 pound processed cheese food (Velveeta), cubed
1 (11-oz.) can condensed cream of cheese soup
2-1/2 c. milk
½ c. sour cream
Fresh chives, chopped (optional)

Brown ground beef in a large, deep skillet over medium-high heat. Drain, crumble and set aside in a bowl. In the same pan simmer carrots, celery, onion and broth for about 10 minutes or until soft. Add rice, mixed vegetables, beef, Velveeta, cheese soup and milk. Cook until cheese is melted, about 5 minutes, stirring frequently. Do not boil. Top with a dollop of sour cream and sprinkle with chives (if desired) just before serving. Serves 6.

LO-CARB CLAM CHOWDER

8 pieces bacon
½ c. finely chopped onion
½ c. finely chopped celery
½ c. finely chopped green pepper (optional)
2 cans clams (6-1/2 oz. each), drained and with the juice reserved
1 c. chicken broth
2 large turnips, peeled and chopped into small cubes (optional)
½ tsp. pepper
½ tsp. dried thyme
Salt
1 c. heavy cream

continued...

SENIOR WANT AD: *"Recent widow who has just buried fourth husband, am looking for someone to round out a six-unit plot. Dizziness, fainting, shortness of breath, not a problem."*

"Never kick a cow chip on a hot day." – <u>Will Rogers</u>

LO-CARB CLAM CHOWDER continued...

Fry the bacon and set it aside, reserving the bacon grease. Sauté the onion, celery and green pepper in 3T. of the bacon grease until they're soft. Remove the onion, celery and green pepper from the heat, and add the clam juice, chicken broth, turnips, pepper, thyme, and salt. Cover and cook over medium heat, stirring occasionally, until the turnips are soft (about 15 minutes). Remove from the heat and stir in the heavy cream and clams. Crumble the bacon and add it to the soup. Reheat over a low flame, and serve. Yield: 4 servings, each with 11 grams of usable carbs.

The sharp or bitter part of the turnip is the outside layer near the skin. Peel your turnips with a paring knife, being careful to get all of the outer layer.

LOW CARB ONION SPICY SOUP

I changed a few recipes around and came up with this great tasting soup. I love it!

Caramelize 2 large onions sliced, with a small amount of olive oil.
Add salt, pepper, red pepper, thyme (to taste) and a small amount of diet sugar. This will take about 15 minutes or more. Add garlic cloves – as many as you like. Add about 2-1/2 cups of low sodium chicken broth. Simmer for about 15 minutes or more. Ladle onions into blender or food processor until smooth. Add back to broth and add whipping cream. Yum, yum!!

KEKKONEN'S CHOWDER
Submitted by Robert Schmid

The late Finnish President Urho Kekkonen especially liked the chowder named after him. A specialty of the district of Kainuu where the president lived as a young boy.

Dice peeled potatoes and put into hot water. Add quartered onions, a bay leaf, whole allspice and salt. Cook the potatoes until almost done. Add large pieces of fish, salmon, whitefish or turbot, and dabs of butter. Cook until the fish is done. If you like, thicken the soup

Kainuu style with a bit of rye flour or leave it clear. Sprinkle with plenty of diced dill and chives. Serve and let each person add finely chopped onions and melted butter.

AVOCADO LO CARB SOUP
A quick and elegant first course

1 large or 2 small, very ripe avocados, pitted, peeled, and cut into chunks
1 qt. chicken broth, heated

Put the avocados through the blender with the broth, puree until very smooth, and serve. Yield: 6 servings.
Total of 2 grams of usable carbs.

If you like curry, try this: Melt a tablespoon or so of butter and add ½ tsp. or so of curry powder. Cook for just a minute and add the mixture to the blender with the broth or avocados. Or try thyme.

SPINACH CHOWDER
1 pkg. (10 oz.) frozen chopped spinach, thawed
2 cans (6-1/2 oz. each) minced clams, including the liquid
1 c. half-and-half
1 c. heavy cream
1 c. water
Salt and pepper

Put the spinach, clams, half-and-half, cream, and water in a blender or food processor, and puree. Pour the mixture into a saucepan, and bring to a simmer (use very low heat and don't boil). Simmer for 5 minutes. Add salt and pepper.

4 servings. 10 grams of usable carbs.

June 4, 1914....Adolph Swanson has purchased an auto, which he brought in from Hibbing Friday evening of last week. This is the first automobile to be brought into the Bear River country.
Bear River Journal

"Don't squat with your spurs on." **Will Rogers**

MANHATTAN STYLE FISH CHOWDER
Mike Borovac's recipe

2 T. butter
2-3/4 c. chopped onion
1 c. chopped carrots
¾ c. chopped celery
3 garlic cloves, minced
¼ c. tomato paste
1 c. dry white wine

2 c. chopped peeled red potatoes
2 c. water
1 tsp. thyme
1 tsp. salt
½ tsp. black pepper
2-8 oz. bottles clam juice
1-28 oz. can diced tomatoes, undrained
1 bay leaf

2 pounds halibut, cod or perch fillets, skinned and cut into 1" pieces.

Melt butter; add onion, carrot, celery and garlic. Sauté 10 minutes. Stir in tomato paste and cook 1 minute. Stir in wine, cook 1 minute. Add potatoes and next 7 ingredients. Bring to a boil. Reduce heat, simmer for 30 minutes. Add fish, cover and simmer 10 minutes or until fish flakes easily. Discard bay leaf.

CHICKEN OF THE FOREST SOUP
Jimmy (Urby) Johnson sent me this recipe using partridge.

1 full partridge (chicken of the forest) – full bird not just the breast
1-1/2 c. celery, chopped
1-1/2 c. carrots, chopped
1-1/2 c. onion, chopped
4 bay leaves
Salt and pepper
½ box dumpling egg noodles
4 T. chicken bouillon granules
½ c. butter
2 qts. water

Continued...

CHICKEN OF THE FOREST SOUP continue...

Simmer partridge in the 2 quarts of water with the bay leaves for 2 hours. Skim off surface.

Cool and separate meat from bones and cut breast in small pieces.

Add celery, carrots, onions, bouillon, butter, salt and pepper to the stock water and simmer for another hour.

Add chicken and keep warm.

Cook noodles, drain, stir in a little butter.

Serve noodles in individual bowls and top with the "Chicken of the Forest Soup". Leftover soup freezes well. Rice can be substituted for the noodles.

SPINACH ONION SOUP

Saute 3 small minced onions and garlic to taste in butter.

Cook 4 c. frozen spinach and 1/3 c. chicken base in 3 quarts of water.

Add cooked spinach to onions. Add chicken base and water and heat. Add two 8 oz. packages of cream cheese in chunks to soup. Add salt, pepper and nutmeg to taste.

VENISON TACO SOUP

1 pound ground venison
1 16-oz. can refried beans (or mashed pinto beans)
1 16-oz.or 24 oz. jar salsa
1 15-oz. can black beans
1 13-oz. can beef broth

Brown venison in a large pot and drain excess grease. Stir in the refried beans. Add remaining ingredients and stir until heated through.

Families are like fudge....mostly sweet, with a few nuts.

I saw a woman wearing a sweatshirt with "Guess" on it...so I said "Implants?"

HAMBURGER SOUP

3 T. butter
1 medium onion, chopped
2 pounds ground beef
4 celery tops
1-28 oz. can tomatoes
3-14.5 oz. can beef consommé, plus 2 cans water
½ tsp. thyme
4 carrots, diced
1 bay leaf
10 peppercorns
½ c. barley
1 can black beans, drained (optional)

Melt butter in a large soup kettle. Sauté onion. Add beef and cook until slightly browned. Add all remaining ingredients, except barley and beans. Bring to a boil. Add barley and cook over medium heat, stirring occasionally for about one hour. Add beans and heat through. Remove celery tops before serving.

Serves 8 to 10.

WORDS OF WISDOM:
When you have a tension headache, do what it says on the aspirin bottle; take two and keep away from children.

Social Security is a strange name for what they actually send you – you can't afford to be social nor can you really feel secure.

A fine is a tax for doing wrong.
A tax is a fine for doing right.

Salads

Son Scott Abel, the love of my life. He & wife Sarah are successful chiropractors in Sauk Centre. They have three boys Gunnar, Cedric and Dieter.

ASIAN SPINACH SALAD
8 T. olive oil
3 T. sugar
3 T. unseasoned rice vinegar
3 T. soy sauce
1-3 oz. package Ramen noodles, coarsely broken
½ c. slivered almonds
2 T. sesame seeds
1-10 oz. spinach
1 bunch green onions, chopped

Whisk 6 T. oil, add rest of ingredients. Add salt and pepper. Heat remaining 2 T. oil. Add noodles (reserve seasoning packet for another use), nuts and sesame seeds. Stir until noodles are toasted and golden about 8 minutes. Pour into large bowl and cool 10 minutes. Add spinach and green onions and toss dressing.

SPICY BACON BITS
Use this in any salad – it sure perks it up!

1 T. Worcestershire sauce
1-1/2 tsp. firmly packed brown sugar
1/8 tsp. cayenne pepper
1/8 tsp. ground allspice
Black pepper to taste
½ pound lean bacon, cut into ¼" squares

Combine all ingredients and add chopped bacon and toss until bacon is well coated. Place in large skillet over medium heat. Cook stirring often until the bacon is crisp, about 10 minutes. Transfer to a paper towel. This will keep in the refrigerator for three days.

Lars asked Ole, "Do ya know da difference between a Norvegian and a canoe?" "No," replied Ole. "A canoe will sometimes tip," explained Lars.

BLUEBERRY SALAD

Cousin Karen Toppson Annala from Duluth brought this to our Finnish reunion – it was great! Just finished having this for lunch.

Wash greens and assemble on plates. Sprinkle with crumbled blue cheese, fresh blueberries and spicy pecans (recipe follows) or use packaged glazed walnuts. Top with maple dressing. Serves 6 to 8.

SPICY PECANS

1 T. ground cinnamon
½ tsp. salt
1 tsp. allspice
2 tsp. sugar
2 T. melted butter

1 tsp. white pepper
½ tsp. red cayenne pepper
¼ tsp. ground ginger
3 c. pecan pieces

Preheat oven to 350 degrees. Spread pecan pieces on cookie sheet and roast for 15 minutes, stirring about every 5 minutes. Spread the mixture on a cookie sheet and let dry for about an hour.

MAPLE DRESSING

1/3 c. apple cider vinegar
¼ c. minced onion
2/3 c. maple syrup
1 T. brown mustard
1 c. canola oil

Place all ingredients together and whisk briskly. Can put in blender also.

Yield: 6-8 servings.

CRUNCHY CHINESE PORK SALAD

4 slices bacon
¾ lb. cubed cooked pork
6 c. torn iceberg lettuce
1-8 oz. can sliced water chestnuts, drained
½ c. sliced green onions
3 T. soy sauce
2 T. honey
1 T. catsup
1 tsp. dry mustard
1-3 oz. can chow mein noodles

continued...

CRUNCHY CHINESE PORK SALAD continued...

In a large skillet, cook bacon till crisp; drain and crumble bacon. In a large bowl combine bacon, pork, lettuce, water chestnuts and green onions. Cover and refrigerate 2-3 hours. For dressing, in a screw-top jar combine soy sauce, honey, catsup and dry mustard. Cover and shake well. Chill. At serving time, add dressing and chow mein noodles to salad, tossing lightly to coat. Serve immediately. Serves 4.

CHEDDAR BROCCOLI SALAD

6 c. fresh broccoli florets
1-1/2 c. (6 oz.) shredded cheddar cheese
1/3 c. chopped onion
1-1/2 c. mayonnaise
¾ c. sugar
3 T. red wine vinegar or cider vinegar
12 bacon strips, cooked and crumbled

Combine the broccoli, cheese and onion. Combine the mayonnaise, sugar and vinegar; pour over mixture and toss to coat. Refrigerate for at least 4 hours. Stir in bacon just before serving. Serves 8.

ELEGANT ROMAINE SALAD

I put together several recipes for this salad – it is excellent! Serves 4

¾ c. Roquefort cheese
3 T. unsalted butter, softened
3 oz. cream cheese, softened
1 package of Romaine lettuce

Blend first three ingredients until smooth. Spread each Romaine leaf with above mixture and press another leaf on top of it. Wrap and chill until time to serve. Chill four plates. Use two leaves per person or accordingly. Sprinkle spicy bacon bits (see recipe) and a slice of a red pear on each leaf. Toast walnuts and sprinkle if desired. Drizzle with a sweet vinaigrette.

PEANUT BUTTER SALAD

This is a salad that the kids will love.

½ c. mayonnaise
2 T. crunchy peanut butter
1 small head green cabbage (4 cups shredded)
1 c. miniature marshmallow
1 red apple cored and chopped
½ c. salted peanuts

Combine mayonnaise and peanut butter, mixing until smooth. Set aside. Combine remaining ingredients. Add mayonnaise and peanut butter mixture, mixing well. Refrigerate at least one hour before serving. Makes 8 servings.

ORIENTAL COLE SLAW

I know this an old recipe, but I love it and always lose the recipe.

1 pkg. beef ramen noodles
1 bag cole slaw mix
1 bunch chopped green onions
1 c. oil
1/3 c. apple cider vinegar
½ c. sugar
1 c. cashews
1 c. sunflower nuts

Combine cole slaw, crunched up ramen noodles, onions and cashews. Combine in separate bowl: oil, vinegar, sugar and seasoning packet from ramen noodles. Toss everything together 1 hour before serving. Serves 8-10.

PISTACHIO PINEAPPLE DELIGHT

This is a favorite recipe from the 1970's and can be either served as a dessert or a salad.

2 pkg. (4-serving size each) Jell-O Pistachio Flavor Instant Pudding & Pie Filling
2 cans (20 oz. each) crushed pineapple in juice, undrained
2 c. Jet-Puffed Miniature Marshmallows
1 c. chopped pecans
3 c. (8 oz. tub) thawed cool whip

continued...

PISTACHIO PINEAPPLE DELIGHT continued...

Mix dry pudding mix, pineapple, marshmallows and pecans in large bowl until well blended. Gently stir in whipped topping; cover. Refrigerate 1 hour or until ready to serve. Makes 16 servings, about ½ cup each.

LEMON CAESAR SALAD

This is a great tasting dressing – use it for a dip for vegetables.

1 small lemon
½ c. light mayonnaise
½ c. Parmesan cheese
2 cloves garlic, minced
3 c. large croutons
Freshly group pepper to taste
Grate peel from lemon; squeeze juice into small bowl. Stir in mayonnaise, ¼ c. cheese and garlic until smooth. (I put all the cheese in with the mayonnaise.) Place lettuce and croutons in large salad bowl. Toss with dressing until well coated. Sprinkle with remaining cheese and pepper. Serves 6.

PECAN-PEAR SALAD

1 large ripe red pear, sliced
2 T. butter or margarine, divided
½ c. coarsely chopped pecans
¼ tsp. salt, divided
2 c. mixed salad greens
2 T. balsamic or red wine vinegar
2 T. olive oil
Pepper to taste

In a large skillet, sauté pear in 1T. butter until lightly browned, about 7 minutes. In another skillet, sauté pecans in remaining butter until lightly browned, about 5 minutes; sprinkle with 1/8-tsp. salt. Divide salad greens between two salad plates; arrange pears over greens. Sprinkle with pecans. Combine the dressing and shake well. Drizzle over salad. Serves 2.

In the 1920's, Shower's Store (now the Side Lake Store) would come to your cabin and get your food order and deliver the next day.

Willpower: *The ability to eat only one salted peanut.*

SPINACH SALAD
Try this sweet dressing for a change of taste!

½ c. oil
¼ c. cider vinegar
¼ c. brown sugar
¼ c. maple syrup
¼ tsp. dry mustard

Add dressing to spinach leaves, red onions, cooked and crumbled bacon, red grapes cut in half.

SPINACH PEAR SALAD
3 c. baby spinach
3 medium ripe yellow pears, cored but not peeled, and cut lengthwise into slices
2 T. crumbled blue cheese

Dressing:
2 T. balsamic vinegar
3 T. extra virgin olive oil
3 T. orange juice
Salt, to taste
1 clove crushed garlic
¼ c. chopped walnuts

In a salad bowl, place spinach, pears and cheese. Whisk together dressing ingredients except walnuts and toss with salad. Toast walnuts 5 minutes in a 325 degree oven. Sprinkle walnuts, while warm over salad. Serves 4.

PEAR SALAD
Same as above, omit the purple onion and add blue cheese to taste and diced pear. Sauté noodles with walnuts, same method as above. Use Good Seasons salad dressing made with olive oil and balsamic vinegar. Add 1T. sugar to dressing and mix well.

STILL ONE OF THE BEST SALADS
Have to bring a salad to a party, this is it!

Layer in this order:
½ cauliflower, pulled apart in small pieces
1 head of lettuce, shredded
Bacon pieces fried and drained
Sliced red onions
1/3 c. mayonnaise (not Miracle Whip) – spread over entire salad
1/3 c. Parmesan cheese sprinkled over mayonnaise
1/3 c. sugar sprinkled over cheese

Cover and refrigerate.

STRAWBERRY SALAD
Brother-in-law Ron Sundquist's favorite

1 pkg. lettuce or romaine
Sliced strawberries to taste
Sliced purple onion to taste
Poppy seed dressing

Sauté one package ramen noodles and ½ cup almonds with 2 T. butter until brown, last 5 minutes before brown add 2 T. sugar to coat evenly, cool before adding to salad. Mix all together just before serving. Chicken may be added.

SWEET AND SOUR CHICKEN SALAD
2/3 c. sour cream
6 T. mayonnaise
2 T. white vinegar
3 T. apricot jam
3 green onions, chopped finely
6 fresh apricots, pitted and diced
1 c. chopped celery
4 boneless, cold, cooked chicken breasts, diced
½ tsp. salt, pepper to taste
Lettuce leaves (use romaine, iceberg, or leaf)

continued...

Salads

SWEET AND SOUR CHICKEN SALAD continued...

In a large bowl, whisk together sour cream, mayonnaise, vinegar and jam. Add green onion, apricots, celery and chicken and toss until evenly coated. Chill and serve over lettuce leaves. Makes 4 servings.

SESAME CHICKEN SALAD

2 boneless chicken breast halves, cooked and cubed
1 c. mayonnaise
1 T. sesame oil
1 T. white sugar
1/8 tsp. ground ginger
1 head Napa cabbage
2 green onions, chopped
1 T. sesame seeds, toasted
1 carrot, shredded
½ c. crispy fried rice noodles, for garnish

To toast sesame seeds, spread in a dry frying pan and place over high heat, stirring constantly until just golden brown.

Several hours before serving, make the dressing by combining the mayonnaise, sesame oil, sugar and ginger. Cover and refrigerate. Thinly slice the cabbage and place in a large bowl along with the cubed chicken. Add the green onion, toasted sesame seeds and shredded carrot. Mix in the dressing and toss. Divide salad onto serving plates and top with additional green onion and crispy rice noodles. Makes 4 servings.

STUFFED TOMATOES

From Roy Ulrich of Virginia – he grows the tomatoes in his garden.

1 pint cherry tomatoes
4 oz. Maytag Blue Cheese
1 T. olive oil
1 T. red wine vinegar
3 T. minced ion
1 T. oregano

Slice tops of tomatoes and remove seeds. Set upside down on paper towels to dry. Mix blue cheese, olive oil, vinegar and onion and stuff into tomatoes. Dust with oregano, cover with saran wrap and chill for ½ hour in refrigerator. Serves 2 to 4.

BLUE CHEESE SALAD DRESSING
Roy Ulrich, Virginia

4 oz. blue cheese (Maytag brand preferred)
4 T. Top the Tater with chives
2 T. milk or half and half

PARTY SALAD
Still ranks up there – an old standby!

Layer in this order:
½ cauliflower, pulled apart in small pieces
1 head of lettuce, shredded
Bacon pieces fried and drained
Sliced red onions
1/3 c. mayonnaise (not Miracle Whip) – spread over entire salad
1/3 c. Parmesan cheese sprinkled over mayonnaise
1/3 c. sugar sprinkled over cheese
Cover and refrigerate.

Finely grate 1 tsp. zest from an orange, then squeeze enough juice to measure 5 tablespoons. Boil 4 T. orange juice with shallot in a very small heavy saucepan over moderate heat, stirring occasionally, until juice is almost evaporated, 4 to 5 minutes. Transfer shallot to a bowl to cool, then stir in zest, mayonnaise, lemon juice, pepper, and remaining tablespoon orange juice. Chill, covered, 1 hour (for flavors to develop).

Minnesota Rurals: "You can bring Coke into my house but it better be brown, wet, and served over ice."

Life is not a journey to the grave with the intention of arriving safely in a pretty and well preserved body, but rather to skid in broadside, thoroughly used up, totally worn out and loudly proclaiming – "WOW, WHAT A RIDE."

Cooking Tips

1. After stewing a chicken, cool in broth before cutting into chunks; it will have twice the flavor.

2. To slice meat into thin strips, as for stir--fry dishes, partially freeze it so it will slice more easily.

3. A roast with the bone in will cook faster than a boneless roast. The bone carries the heat to the inside more quickly.

4. When making a roast, place dry onion soup mix in the bottom of your roaster pan. After removing the roast, add 1 can of mushroom soup and you will have a good brown gravy.

5. For a juicier hamburger, add cold water to the beef before grilling (½ cup to 1 pound of meat).

6. To freeze meatballs, place them on a cookie sheet until frozen. Place in plastic bags. They will stay separated so that you may remove as many as you want.

7. To keep cauliflower white while cook-ing, add a little milk to the water.

8. When boiling corn, add sugar to the water instead of salt. Salt will toughen the corn.

9. To ripen tomatoes, put them in a brown paper bag in a dark pantry, and they will ripen.

10. To keep celery crisp, stand it upright in a pitcher

11. When cooking cabbage, place a small tin cup or can half full of vinegar on the stove near the cabbage. It   will absorb the odor.

12. Potatoes soaked in salt water for 20 minutes before baking will bake more rapidly.

13. Let raw potatoes stand in cold water for at least a half-hour before frying in order to improve the crispness of French-fried potatoes. Dry potatoes thoroughly before adding to oil.

14. Use greased muffin tins as molds when baking stuffed green peppers.

15. A few drops of lemon juice in the water will whiten boiled potatoes.

16. Buy mushrooms before they "open." When stems and caps are attached firmly, mushrooms are truly fresh.

17. Do not use metal bowls when mixing salads. Use wood, glass or china.

18. Lettuce keeps better if you store it in the refrigerator without washing it. Keep the leaves dry. Wash lettuce the day you are going to use it.

19. Do not use soda to keep vegetables green. It destroys Vitamin C.

20. Do not despair if you over salt gravy. Stir in some instant mashed potatoes to repair the damage. Just add a little more liquid in order to offset the thickening.

Stories

Mona and Kevin Mchale, Side Lake 4th of July Parade Story on page 138

KEVIN MCHALE – OUR NEIGHBOR IN SIDE LAKE

Kevin and his family are part time residents of Side Lake and when they show up at the local establishments, the locals all say hello and leave him alone.

On an infamous 4th of July Side Lake Parade in 1989, Kevin was Snow White and I was "Happy" – one of the seven dwarfs.. To quote Eleanor Ostman, writer for the St. Paul Pioneer Press (friend of mine since first grade), she wrote in June of 1990, "Nobody has more fun on the Fourth of July than the people of Side Lake, a lake-cabin community north of Chisholm. Drawing an estimated 5,000 spectators each year, the Side Lake parade stars such groups as the Happy Tappers and The Perch Lake Drill Team. They carry variable-speed drills, braces and bits. The Side Lake area's most famous summer resident, Boston Celtics star and Hibbing native Kevin McHale, has been known to join the parade. Last year, McHale sashayed the parade route as Snow White in a long formal dress and black wig, surrounded by seven "dwarves". (Almost anyone qualifies as a dwarf standing next to McHale.) They don't say that Kevin's in the parade. They just happened to have a 6-foot 10-inch Snow White."

After the parade, Snow White and the seven dwarfs were at Riverside having a few 7-ups (of course Kevin had to buy) and I said, "Hey, Snow, wait until we get you home". I cannot print what he said, just use your imagination.

AHO'S POOL HALL (HIBBING)

Taken from Dick Marinucci's cookbook "Treasures of the North Woods". Tilly (as we call him) resides in Walker, MN.

"On into the eleventh and twelfth grades the gathering place became the curling club or the Pool Hall. The Pool Hall was full of colorful characters from ages 12 to 80. We learned to play pool fairly well, but soon we wised up and took on only the ones we could beat or at least not have to pay for the game. The Pool Hall offered a nice form of "education" that was not available in school books. It paralleled the skating shack where we first learned how to swear correctly. The Pool Hall was a graduate course where we learned about girls, baseball, hunting, fishing, pool, fighting and a host of other things that were necessary to function as an adult on the "Iron Range".

Junior Milovich would occasionally grace the premises on a Friday night. His brother Ritchy owned the cab company and the Dox tavern next door to the Pool Hall. Junior was usually drunk and disorderly when he arrived. This, coupled with the fact he was strong and crazy, gave you reason to get out of the way. The safest place was under a pool table because soon he was throwing pool balls at people and trying to spear them with cue sticks. When he came through the door, Mike Aho would just call the police to come and subdue him.

continued...

AHO'S POOL HALL (HIBBING) continued...

The strongest guy in town, Stevie Furin, was like Jeckl and Hyde. He only drank on the weekend, and he was middle aged. He lived with his mother in an apartment above one of the businesses on 1ˢᵗ Avenue. He was stocky, only about 5'8" with broad shoulders. Occasionally, we would see him in the dead of winter dressed in a muscle shirt with bare feet walking to the liquor store a half block away. He had a high pitched voice and hardly said a word when he was sober. He would come into the bar, put his arm across it, walk to the end collecting all the glasses as he went, and throw them on the floor. People just moved away and let him do it. Then he would announce in his squeaky voice, "No one in the house can lick Stevie Furin". Nobody tried.

Stevie was barred from the bowling alley because he would throw the balls so hard it would split the pins.

One night in front of the L and B Café, he lifted up the back end of a Studebaker car. At the Dox Bar, one night, we heard sirens and came out of the Pool Hall as three cops rushed into the Dox. One came out, when he saw it was Stevie, he called for help. Altogether, seven cops finally got him in the car. They couldn't handcuff him because his wrists were too big for cuffs. Stevie was one tough fella.

ERWIN LESTER CAIN

Uncle Erwin was my Grandmother Edith Cain Williams' brother. His son Richard sent this to me:

"I'll always remember the time my dad made some cookies. I was about five or six years old. I could hardly wait until they were done. As soon as they were cool my dad gave me one. It was the hottest cookie I had ever eaten. He had mistakenly used cayenne pepper instead of cinnamon."

Erwin was born in Ishpeming on February 4, 1894. Erwin quit school after grade 10 and went to work in the underground mine, but broke his big toe. His dad told him to stay out of the mines because he worked in them and never liked it.So he headed out to Detroit to work at the Ford plant, but he came down with smallpox and returned home to recuperate. His father caught the smallpox from him and died. He stayed home to be with his mother. After she passed away, he packed up and headed for Hibbing. It was in the early 1920's.

He lived with my grandmother and grandfather as they took in boarders and lived there until he married.

A story I like to tell, is one morning Erwin got up and said to my grandfather, "What was that commotion last night"? He said, "Oh, Edith had a baby". It was the birth of my aunt Priscilla (Perky). He didn't even know she was pregnant.

After working construction he went to work at the Central Laundry in 1926 until 1951. He passed away in 1955 at the age of 61 years old.

BOB (ZIMMERMAN) DYLAN

Bob was a graduate of Hibbing High School in 1959 and went on to worldwide fame. Everyone knows his accomplishments, but did you know he use to call my sister Carole and play the guitar and sing his songs? Carole was in 8th grade and Bob was in 10th grade. He would call with an alias name (she can't remember the name he used) and he would play and sing songs. Carole would just listen and then tell him what she thought of his songs. She related to me, that they were all very good songs. This would be for 15 minutes to ½ hour several times a week. At this time in his life, he was playing the piano, not the guitar.

When Carole would see him on Friday nights standing by Bridgeman's on Howard Street, he would ignore her.

The question is, did he call other girls and sing to them, or was it only Carole? Only Bob knows!

HUGH CASEY

The following is the second place winner Kasey Karasti, Hugh Casey's granddaughter, who wrote the following essay in the Voice of Democracy contest at Hibbing High School.

"I come from a very large family of veterans. I am very fortunate to be the daughter of a Vietnam veteran and the granddaughter of three World War II veterans. They are all amazing stories of bravery and heroism, but the one I would like to tell is of my grandfather, Hugh Casey, who was a P.O.W. in World War II.

My grandpa went for his physical and found out he was 4F, which means he was medically unable to serve in the military because of his allergies. He refused to be labeled this. So his dad found a specialist in Minneapolis and got him cleared to enlist. Then he hurried to get his physical for the service.

He started his service into the Army Air Corps on June 30, 1943. My grandpa was to be a tail gunner on a B-17 flying fortress bomber . His first mission was to bomb an oil field south of Leipzig in eastern Germany. His plane was shot down on that mission and he was shot in both of his legs. He parachuted out and landed in a tree and some farmers' wives started beating him with sticks. Boys from the Hitler Youth Organization captured him. They got him out of the tree, and because he couldn't walk, they dislocated both of his arms. Now as you can imagine my grandpa was in really tough shape. I mean he couldn't walk, move his arms and didn't have any hearing as a result of being shot down. After some time he was dragged to a train station and thrown in a cattle car.

continued...

After a couple of weeks of being moved from place to place, without any medical help, my grandpa was finally transported to Berlin, where he received the help he needed. Then my grandpa was transported to Frankfurt, Germany. His interrogator was a German officer who spoke excellent English. My grandpa only gave him his name, rank and serial number. The officer had a clipboard and on it was very detailed information about my grandpa and his family's life. It turned out that this soldier had lived in Duluth and spent some time on the Iron Range as a drug salesman, and even spent some time in Chisholm, and had been in my great-grandpa's drugstore. However my grandpa never saw this officer again.

My grandpa was liberated by General Patton, who shook his splinted arms and pinned a Purple Heart to his pillow. That day he was sent to New York City in a body cast and weighed under 100 pounds including the cast.

Throughout his years, when I was around, I could see how his injuries would affect his daily life. My grandpa was very patriotic until the day he died and because of this he was thankful for every day he spent on American soil, and never regretted serving for his country. He is one I will admire and respect forever."

THE FRABONI BROTHERS – LEO and ANGELO

Leo and Angelo came from a very strong Italian immigrant family.

Their father hated working in the mines, so in 1927 he bought a grocery/butcher store in Brooklyn (a suburb of Hibbing) and started making homemade garlic sausages. To this day, they are the best!

By 1949, Leo and Angelo were wholesaling the sausage. In 1955 Angelo was making porketta's the way they made them in Italy. Nobody knew what they were at that time except the old time Italians. One of the main ingredients in porketta is fresh fennel (there are 27 varieties). At one time everyone in Brooklyn was growing fennel for Fraboni's.

Both Leo and Angelo are gone, but new owners are carrying on the tradition of the Fraboni family.

Check out their website to order their delicious products! **www.frabonis.com**

This poem was written by Gail Williams Farnham's mother, Toborg "Toby" E. Wiliams. She died February 10, 2003.

THE LAST RACE

Time, please stop and wait for me
I'm trying to keep up, can't you see?
All these tasks just must be done
Some of which I've just begun.

Dogeared pages, books unread
Letters half written, words unsaid
Too late now, as I didn't know then
Your grasp was faster than my pen.

Snapshots, clippings in disarray
Waiting for that rainy day
The tooth the fairy clean forgot
A lock of hair it means a lot.

Organdy pinafores never sewn
Now she's children of her own
Golden plaques of little hands
Crayon drawings in rubber bands.

Drawers to clean, clothes to mend
Seems that there will be no end.
The telephone rings, "I'm so lonely"
"I'll come but for a minute only".

The day did come but t'was too late
She's already entered the pearly gate
But patiently there she waits for me
To join her in timeless eternity.

Time, not so fast, hear my plea
Hills are steeper than they used to be
I falter now with each step I take
I pray be patient for my sake.

When I say I have no time
Why do I waste it on this rhyme?
Alas, no use, I'll never catch up
So time, you've won the coveted cup.

(This could have been written for my mother.)

BOOTLEGGING ON THE RANGE
By Z.A.(Knobby) Valeri

"There were four bootleggers in Hibbing that used to drive to New Orleans to pick up liquor. This was sold to private parties, private clubs and one local drug store that sold liquor.

There was a club downstairs of Rano's pool hall that sold alcohol. This was next to where the Old Howard is now. Just before every dance, all the fellows would go down to buy a pint to take to the dance. We then went to Stein's Drugstore and bought prescription bottles, we filled them up with alcohol and packed them in suitcases, stashed it in the back of my dad's car and went selling.

Believe it or not, we parked the car in the police station parking lot. We had overcoats so we could put a pint in each pocket, and a couple in our pants pockets. We then took off for the front to Rano's pool hall.

When a guy would start for the downstairs of Rano's, we would approach him and ask if he was looking for booze. If he said yes, we'd offer them ours for $.50 a pint. Other people were charging $2 a pint.

I always reflect on how many children were clothed, fed and educated on money earned by selling liquor. You must remember in those early days there was no AFDC, no relief money and no help from government agencies..... I remember one particular widow who lived on the corner of Second Avenue East and Portage Street (now 25th Street) who had a regular route she covered every other day. They called her Suitcase Agnes because she carried a suitcase filled with pints and quarts of liquor and delivered it to various steady customers...I used to deliver for one of the big bootleggers. I used my father's 1930 Ford 2-door sedan. I delivered five gallon crook jugs wrapped in a gunny sack. I had the back seat out of the car and got four of those jugs in the back. I can remember my customers well. There was Joe Y., Jim M., Sadie P. and Mrs. K at the Morris Location....Mr. Viitala was the federal agent for 28 years. His biggest bust was the still in North Hibbing at the Day Lake area....it was then shipped to a distribution point in Moorhead as the production was more than they could use locally.

There were quite a few individuals involved and it was rumored that one of the head medical doctors in Hibbing was a very big investor. When the ring was raided and the operation shut down, the only people that were arrested and sent to jail were the workers. None of the investors were ever sent to jail or arrested.

***Reprinted in part from an article in the
Sunday, January 4, 2004, "The Daily Tribune"***

ITALIAN COOKIES

Jimmy (Urby) Johnson of Hibbing sent me this story.

An elderly Italian man lay dying in his bed. While suffering the agonies of impending death, he suddenly smelled the aroma of his favorite Italian anisette sprinkled cookies wafting up the stairs. He gathered his remaining strength and lifted himself from the bed. Leaning against the wall, he slowly made his way out of the bedroom, gripping the railing with both hands, he crawled downstairs.

He would have thought himself already in heaven, for there, spread out on the kitchen table were literally hundreds of his favorite anisette cookies.
Was it heaven or one final act of heroic love from his devoted Italian wife of sixty years.

Mustering one great final effort, he threw himself towards the table, landing on his knees in a crumpled posture. The aged and withered hand trembled on its way to a cookie at the edge of the table, when it was suddenly smacked with wooden spoon by his wife.....

"Back off!", she said, "They're for the funeral."

Minnesotans are just different, that's all. On the day of which I speak, with the wind-chill factor hovering at fifty-seven below, hundreds of them could be perceived through the slits of my ski mask out ice fishing on this frozen lake. It was cold out there, bitter, biting, cutting, piercing, hyperborean, marmoreal cold, and there were all these Minnesotans running around outdoors, happy as lambs in spring.

From Charles Kuralt's book "Dateline America"

HOW STINGY LAKE WAS NAMED

As told by Mary Spotts in her book "***Stingy Lake Country***"

"Twenty years or more before the turn of the century, surveyors were sent out to map and measure the land. They had the authority to name lakes. Often they were out for days at a time without the benefit of a good camp cook. Salt pork and beans was oft their daily fair, plus wild meat.

The surveyors were in the wilderness many days when they approached a calm, clear blue lake. It was a pleasant and beautiful sight. That was not all that pleased them. They recognized the aroma of freshly baked bread. They came upon a cabin occupied by Mr. Woodman. Anticipation of the taste of fresh bread grew as they knocked on the door. Cautiously, Mr. Woodman opened the door a few inches and asked what they wanted. One surveyor said they smelled fresh baked bread and would like to buy a loaf, if possible. Mr. Woodman harshly said it wasn't for sale and quickly closed the door.

Disgruntled by the refusal, they discussed their experience. This beautiful lake, they decided, would be named Stingy Lake instead of Woodman Lake. His abrupt selfish act influenced the naming of the lake."

The 1903 population of Gilbert was 1,300. It had 36 saloons.
Hibbing's population was 5,000 in 1905. It had 66 saloons.

JENO PAULUCCI

Jeno graduated from Hibbing High School in 1935.

A son of Italian immigrants, he is probably best known for his Jeno's make-at-home pizza. However, he also was the first to market packaged Chinese food using the Chun King label in 1947. When he sold Chun King in 1966, he received $63 million dollars in cash. He then concentrated his efforts on his pizza-mix business, which he later sold to Pillsbury for $150 million dollars. It goes on and on, but some small tidbits about the man:

Terry Butorac formerly from Hibbing related: "Jeno was at a meeting in the South with some heavy hitters. They were introduced as John Smith III, Harvard, Jerry Brown, Yale, and when it came to Jeno he said, "Jeno Paulucci, graduate of Hibbing Junior College."

When I was helping Rudy Perpich on his campaign, we had a bar-b-q at our cabin on South Sturgeon. Jeno and his beautiful wife Lois attended. My daughter Melanie started playing catch with him using a bocce ball. Oh boy, I thought, there could be serious consequences here. The following week, Melanie received a nice note and he enclosed a catcher's mitt and soft ball.

Graduate 1935
Hibbing High School
Lincoln Tribune : Lincoln Minstrel "Ask the professor"
"Short of Stature-he truly may be , But a better orator
we never may see."

JACK LEMMON AND MONA

My friend Sally Miller Gordon originally from Hibbing, lived in Palm Springs, California for 20 years.

For many years, the highlight of February or March was going to visit. During many of these visits we would attend the Dinah Shore Open, the day the celebrities would attend and mingle with us common folk.

I thought before one trip, "Oh I hope I get a chance to see Jack Lemmon". I had seen his latest movie, "***The Tribute***" – a story of a man dying and plans his last party. When he got up on the stage he said, "I once had an aunt who thought she was a poached egg".

Yes, I thought, I will say that to him if I see him. Well, my ex and I are strolling the greens when we spot him in a golf cart. Ray said, "Get over there so I can get a picture".

So as he got out of the cart, (I noticed his eyes were rather red and watery) I sputtered "I once had an aunt who thought she was a poached egg". His eyes bulged out of his head, he jumped in his cart and drove 100 miles an hour to the clubhouse.

I am sure he thought I was a nut case. At the clubhouse he ran inside for perhaps a half an hour and then came out and visited with all of us. I hung back against the wall so he wouldn't freak out if he saw me, although I still had my picture taken with him. What a time we had!

Jack & Mona

JIMMY (URBY) JOHNSON

Jimmy Johnson sent me several recipes from his childhood and also some very personal stories. Jimmy graduated from Hibbing High School in 1957 and went on to become a teacher in the St. Cloud area. He is now retired and spends a lot of time at his hunting shack North of Side Lake.

" During the hellish strikes of the 1950's, our family had to pull together and enclose to survive. " One thing I remember was the meals and things my mother had to put together to feed the five of us.

Though we had very little personal wealth, my parents would NEVER accept any welfare from the state or individuals. Their pride was something that never wavered, even though at times it brought tears. I can remember things like digging up the wooden street blocks in North Hibbing on dark nights with my dad so we could have heat in our home. I remember living in the metal huts on 4th Avenue West, where the poor lived. Hauling five-gallon buckets of kerosene in the hut each winter morning before school and after doing my paper route. Plus many more things....the weasel I thought was my pet, the hail hitting the tin roof, the ore trains thundering outside our door all day and night. Many images come to mind, but most of all I remember how our small family pulled together in love through the hardest of times. God gave us little in material goods but he made us a loving family and truly we were blessed by his love and grace.

The following are two true recipes that helped fill our stomachs through some hard times."

5-4-7 STEW

During the strike of 1951-52, this stew fed a family of 5 for 7 days (5-4-7 Stew). The cost of this week-long stew was about $2.00, and the $2.00 came from my paper route. Just add water, if you run short.

Salt and pepper
½ c. catsup
1 lbs. carrots, peeled and sliced)
2 lbs. hamburger
3 lbs. onions, chopped
4 bay leaves
5 lbs. potatoes, peeled and sliced

Sauté hamburger and onions in large pot. Add remainder of the ingredients and two gallons of water. Bring to boil and simmer for two hours.

STRIKE-ETTI

1 lb. bacon
2 cans tomato soup
3 lbs. noodles, any kind
Salt and pepper

Fry and cut up bacon until just about crisp. Do not drain. Put in a large pot. Add tomato soup and 2 cans of water. Simmer and stir often. Cook the noodles. Drain and add to bacon and tomato soup sauce. Add salt and pepper. Mix well.

NORBERT ARNOLD

Pengilly, MN now living in Maplewood, MN

See his chokecherry wine in the beverage section. This recipe was given to Mrs. Lucille Method and her husband from Norbert in the 50's when they lived in Hibbing and knew Mr. Arnold. Mrs. Method now lives in Negaunee, Michigan.

Mr. Arnold was a State Senator representing the counties of Itasca, Koochiching, Cass, and Beltrami at various times from 1967 through 1976. He also was quite an inventor and probably invented the first snowmobile and four wheeler. My brother-in-law Ron Sundquist knows him from Pengilly and loved to go over to his garage and see what he was inventing. Ron has one of his "tanks". Mr. Arnold sent me this story about a true Iron Range character, but he changed his name.

"DRAGO"

And then there was Drago who had emigrated from Serbia as a young man. Very little was known about his personal life except that he apparently had no wife or friends and he very rarely spoke to any one in the bar where he was a regular, except the bartender. Every day after work as a laborer in the mines, Drago would enter the bar and proceed to the last stool, which I suspect was deemed by other imbibers as Drago's domain, and start drinking the whiskey, or whatever the bartender had prepared for him as soon as he entered the bar. Drago always wore a hat resembling "Smokey the Bear" hat with a somewhat taller peak, the same jacshirt, the same pants, etc.

Anyway, getting back to Drago, the most interesting thing about him was that during most of the time that he sat at the bar, he told himself jokes and laughed, sometimes raucously.

Nobody ever bothered him and I suspect that he didn't miss the fellowship of other bar patrons. He was self contained.

JOHANNES (JOHN) WILENIUS

JOHANNES (JOHN) was born in 1880 in Messukyla, Hame, Finland to Mikel Edvard Wilenius and his wife Maria Evelina Matintytar. He was the last of six children and at the age of 23 left Liverpool, England on the Carpathia. He arrived in New York on June 30, 1903 and made his way to Chisholm. He became active in the community as athletic director for a gymnastic group in 1908, directed the Chisholm Workers' Society and was a member of the Chisholm City Band. In 1907 he married Eva Hanna Blom in a large wedding for those times.

When the government let out land grants they settled in Sturgeon Township on 160 acres and built a large farmhouse. It has had livestock continuously on this property since 1909 and is now owned and operated by John's son Leo.

The present Sturgeon Town Hall was then School #33 and the Wilenius children attended school there. Older sons John and Swen drove the enclosed wagon to school with wheels in good weather and runners in the winter. The trip to town to get supplies took two days and the men and horses had to cross Sturgeon River twice going through the water before the bridges were built. Mother Eva Hanna would walk the mile and a half to visit Mrs. Vainio and it was a two mile walk to get their mail.

There were big log drives on Sturgeon River and young John, Jr. would go on the day that the wanigan (cook shack float boat) would come and cook for the crew. The early road from Chisholm to Tower went just north on the edge of the homestead in those days and supplies came from either of those towns.

MARIO MICHAEL RETICA

Born to Bernadine and Luca Retica in Hibbing on March 22, 1912 and died on July 7, 1995.

Mario graduated from Hibbing High School, Hibbing Junior College and the College of St. Thomas. Mario was a teacher and coach in Austin, MN from 1937 to 1941. He met his beautiful bride Mary Decker from Austin and they were married in 1938. They moved to Buhl where he taught from 1941 through 1944. Mary didn't quite know how to act like a Ranger, but she was a quick learner.

Hibbing High School was his final destination arriving in 1944 until his retirement in 1976. He was a teacher, coach and athletic director.

Athletic events were the social fabric of the Retica household. The "after game coffee" was a main stay at 615 E. 23rd Street. One of the main stay treats to have with the coffee was the favorite mint brownie.

continued...

MARIO MICHAEL RETICA continued...

After retirement he ran and won as mayor of Hibbing. Mario really got into this new role and now Mary was "first lady". He was mayor for two terms 1976 to 1980. From 1982 until 1988 he held a seat on the city council.

Before he died, I would go over and give him a neck and upper back massage with him sitting at the kitchen table with his head rested on a pillow on the table. This worked the best for him. He liked to make a lot of noise but I think he enjoyed the massage and he was gentle as a lamb.

I bet Mario is tooting that whistle in heaven and bossing around his former students.

DURWOOD OOTHOUDT

Durwood was born in Hibbing in 1917 and passed away in Hibbing in 1991.

Daughter Connie recalls: "My father left my mother Eloise in 1942 to participate in WWII. I was two months old when he left and was four years old when he returned in 1945. My parents found housing across the driveway from the Meittunen family. Durwood worked for US Steel.

My dad drank a lot of coffee – he loved it. I grew up never tasting "bought" bread or cookies. My mother and grandmother Echo were exceptional cooks and bakers.

Despite the fact my dad loved good food, my mother informed me he could not even make a pot of coffee. Then she thought, yes, there was one thing he could make. In the evening, when he had his fill of coffee, he would take a glass of cold milk, add crushed soda cracker and sprinkle with sugar – yum!

My dad was a great sportsman. He loved to fish, hunt and pick blueberries. Every fall he would come home with a big buck, hang it in the garage, skin it, cut it up and haul it into the basement."

The Meittunen family visited often and once my brother Roger (must have been very thirsty) as he sucked the oil out of the heater and had to be rushed to the hospital to have his stomach pumped.

I thought Durwood was such a handsome man!

MESABA PARK IN CHERRY

During my teenage years, a group of us from Iron Junction Road and beyond, would ride our old bicycles to Mesaba Park and go swimming. I think the group consisted of Marilyn Niemi, Sharon Maki, Norm Mattson, Norm Koski, sister Carole,cousin Cheryl and myself.

We knew Mesaba Park was run by the communists, but, of course, we really didn't know what communists were and didn't care.

In 1929 Finnish farmers and workers obtained 240 acres of woods and a 52 acre North Star Lake. It has been used for camping and the pavilion utilized for meetings, dances and concerts.

When "McCarthyism" hit in the 50's, apparently there were FBI agents at the gates taking names and license numbers down. People were afraid to come to the park.

The park was created to provide Finnish people a place to meet and relax. Finns were very active in the early labor organizations and some were blacklisted and couldn't get jobs in the mines and even logging. A lot of those people were members of the park.

A school mate of mine, Kathy Halberg, was the niece of Gus Hall, the president of the Communist Party. He grew up in Cherry. She couldn't get a job with the state or federal government. She went to New York to visit him and he gave her a watch that belonged to Nikita Khruchev.

We had many great times swimming there and as it was about five miles one way, we were always in excellent shape.

The park is still open to the public and they hold many Finnish festivals. At one time the mid-summer party had 8 to 10,000 people in the park.

JOE STUKEL, THE MUSICIAN

Joe was always interested in music, even as a young child. At age five, he saw a man on a street car playing an accordion. He went up to the man and watched him play. He dreamed of getting his own accordion, but that was not possible, for times were tough and there was no extra money.

During Joe's high school years, from many odd jobs, he saved his money and was able to get a used clarinet and later a saxophone.

In years to come, Joe played in the Hibbing concert band and many dance bands which took him to Europe, Hawaii and various states.

In 1996, at Ironworld, Joe was inducted into the Polka Hall of Fame.

Today he is still playing on the Range and he is now in his 90's. Keep up the good job Joe!

1935 Graduate
Hibbing High School
Albert Borelli
Vice-president

Wife Lena and Al
were friends of my parents.

1935 Graduate
Hibbing High School
James Luthen
Co-founder of L&M Supply Co.

Believe in comfort
and moderate ease:
Work when work just
happens to please.

1935 Graduate
Hibbing High School
Gustie Erickson
Jerry Erickson's Father

Basketball; Golf; Hockey; Track;
Large H; Prom Music Committee;
Hi-Y; "H" Club; Junior Minstrels.

*Incomparable... droll... a broad
grin... street-singer...
golf enthusiast...*

MY DAD, JOHN ERIC MEITTUNEN

Dad was born in 1913 in Soudan, Minnesota, the second oldest of immigrant's from Finland.

Dad and Me

He was a very quiet man who worked at construction sites around the Iron Range after he graduated from Chisholm High School in 1931. Until doing this cookbook, I had never seen his graduation picture.

He met my mother Myra Jean Wiliams from Pensobscot when she was in 12th grade (my dad was 5 years older than her). According to mom's diary, she and Johnny went to movies almost every night. They married in 1937.

From the time I was little, dad took me to the movies. My mom had other kids to take care of and there wasn't much money for babysitters. In fact, we never had babysitter's other than family members. Of course, the movies we went to were John Wayne and westerns. I didn't care what they were, I loved going with my dad.

Dad was a great carpenter and mother was the architect. Our house was added on to for 40 years or more.

In the winter dad starting buying wrecked cars and would heat up the garage and work on cars. Of course, my brothers all learned how to take an engine out of a car and put it back. The three girls learned how to be "social butterflies".

Dad worked at the Oliver Mining Company later named US Steel until his retirement in 1975. His business card said "Maintenance Foreman".

Dad was very active in the Shriners, the Engineers Club, and the Methodist Church.

One winter he decided to build a wood boat in the basement. Boy, was he busy. When spring arrived, he and a few friends decided to move it out, but, you guessed it, it wouldn't fit up the stairs and out the door. They had to take the entire steps out. To say the least, there were a few tense moments. My dad didn't swear, but the other men did for him. We didn't dare bring this up for probably 25 years.

What he loved best was their cabin they bought in 1962 on South Sturgeon. Nothing was called work there – it was fun! Of course, 1962 was a big year for the Meittunen family. My mother was 44 and my dad was 49 and mom was carrying twins.

Dad took a lot of kidding at work and was very embarrassed by it all.

continued…

MY DAD, JOHN ERIC MEITTUNEN continued…

He also loved new clothes and new cars. I remember very well the new 1953 Buick Roadmaster he bought. Mom, dad and four kids, drove off to Venice,California to visit mom's sister Perky. As there was no air conditioning at this time, we rented a metal container that was strapped on the driver's window and you filled it with water. You pulled a cord and water cooled the inside of your car. Well, of course, when he drove through Death Valley, the water ran out. Luckily for me, I slept through the entire adventure.

Dad loved us all in his own Finnish way. Actions always spoke louder than words. He died in 1991 at the age of 78. Dad, this book is for you!

NICHOLAS PAUL MARAS….known as Big Nick

Owner of the Homer Bar in Hibbing

Our teddy bear friend Big Nick died at the age of 93 on January 28, 2002. The following are excerpts from this obituary:

"He was born in the Austria-Hungarian province of Croatia to Mata and Mary Maras on December 8, 1908. He came to America in December of 1922 with his mother, sisters and grandparents. He met his father for the first time when he was thirteen years old. He learned English, became an American citizen and graduated from Hibbing High School where he excelled in sports. When Prohibition ended, he went into business with his father opening up the Homer Tavern & Hotel in 1933 that he owned and managed until his death.

He and a friend were invited as walk-ons to join the 1930 Chicago Bears football team, where his friend "Bronco" Nagerski was currently playing. He was possibly the oldest bartender/owner in the United Stated, reporting for work at 6:00 AM each morning."

He was a big man with hands the size of ham hocks and even late in life was known to jump over the bar and grab a customer if that person insulted a woman or was irritating Big Nick.

The Homer Bar was a working man's bar and women did not enter it safely until the 1960's. That was the way it was on the Range.

We all miss you Big Nick, but know that you are at the big bar in the sky!

Paul "Pop" Lukens

Paul Lukens, Hibbing's swimming mentor, and producer of starring teams and starring men. Even world champions have come from Luken's teams and we have no doubt but what bigger and better teams will appear in the future.

– Hematite 1936

Clyde Hill
1935 Graduate
Hibbing High School
The first mayor of South Sturgeon

Hi-Y, vice-president-orchestra director; Band; Orchestra; Glee Club; "Pampered Darling".

The biggest little man in school.

157

RUDY PERPICH – OUR GOVERNOR FROM HIBBING

Our family moved back to Side Lake and Hibbing in 1975 and I became a volunteer for Rudy's campaign for governor in 1977. He was defeated by Republican Al Quie. He ran again and I volunteered again. He won the governorship in 1982 and went on to win two full terms.

I enjoyed the fast pace that went with fundraising and organizing events for Rudy. I also enjoyed going to the mansion for special parties.

Rudy always came to the state high school hockey games in St. Paul and would invite all the "Rangers" to the mansion after the games on Friday and Saturday nights. The servers would carry around trays with glasses of wine for the "Rangers" and Rudy was heard to say, "Give them each a bottle – after all they are Rangers".

Rudy was a tall and imposing figure. My most embarrassing moment in my life was when he asked me to polka at his fundraising birthday party at the Hibbing Memorial Building. Needless to say, I cannot go into detail. My close friends always say, "please, tell that Rudy story to us again".

He was a hard working governor and one great story was when he was driving back up north at 2:00 or 3:00 AM and ran out of gas in Moose Lake. He went to the locked door at the Moose Lake State Hospital (we called it the nut house) and knocked. The man inside opened the small window in the door and Rudy said, "I am Governor Rudy Perpich and I ran out of gas and need help".To which the man said, "And I am Paul Newman" and slammed the window shut.

When he died in 1995 at the age of 67, there was an empty void left in the State of Minnesota and on the Iron Range.

SIDE LAKE'S MINSTREL SHOW

Maxine Simpson, Irene (Lange) Hemphill   Billy Mayer, Dorthy (Mayer) Gross

SAMMY'S PIZZA

The first Sammy's Pizza was opened in Hibbing in 1954 by Sam and Louise Perrella (across the street on Howard Street from where it is now). We were all young, and in our Finnish-English household, we wondered, what is a pizza? On Friday nights we would stand outside of their front window and watch Sam throw the pizza dough. Boy, what excitement!

The original hours were a grueling 4:00 PM to 3:00 AM.

It all started after World War II when some of the G.I.'s who had been overseas remembered the cuisine they had experienced in foreign countries. Some of those vets got to talking one day with Sam Perrella, who owned a little café in Keewatin. Stationed in Italy, they had enjoyed a dish nobody had seen in these parts. It was called pizza.

Sam learned that the pizza was popular in Chicago, so one day he made some contacts and then drove to Chicago. Returning to Keewatin, he talked to his wife Louise who began experimenting with the recipes.

On October 2, 1954, Sammy's Pizza was born and there are now 17 stores throughout Minnesota and Wisconsin.

In the late 70's, Sam passed away and sons Greg and Jeff took over the operations. In 1976, a fire burned the original location and the Perrella's moved across the street.

SIDE LAKE'S MINSTREL SHOW

Every fall beginning in 1952 or 1953, a variety show with skits and vaudeville, would be held at Pine Beach Resort. In charge were Irene Olson, Vera Gunderson and Adeline Potami. Adeline played the piano and Denny Belschner played the accordion.

It was always in black face ala Al Jolson. The black faces were Pete Belschner, Wesley White, Jim Sixberry, David Perry and Billy Sixberry. They would sing a verse. Those in the picture at right are:

Augusta Mayer, Ruth Libke, Richard Potami, Charlie Walters, Ray Potami, Wayne Knoop, and Barbara (Libke) Zaic.

ST. URHO'S DAY
What – you don't know about St. Urho?

On the Iron Range and in Menahga, the day before St. Patrick's Day, the Finnish people celebrate with the patron saint, St. Urho. He drove the grasshoppers from the vineyards of Finland. The tale of how St. Urho's Day came to be is not known. Some credit envious Finns who wanted their own celebration. Others credit boosters in Virginia, MN, home to a sizable Finnish populations. I heard it was Jim Klobuchar, a former Iron Ranger who had a column in the Minneapolis Star. Some speculate St. Urho came into being in the l950's around the same time that Urho Kekkonen became the president of Finland in March, 1956.

In Menahga, they just go nuts! Check out their website goMenahga.com. They have a statue of St. Urho with a grasshopper skewered on a pitchfork. During their ceremony, they chant in Finnish "Heinasirkka, heinasirkka, menetaalta hiiteen," meaning "Grasshopper, grasshopper, go away." Then men in green costumes begin kicking their legs like a grasshopper. Purple is the color of the day.

Boy do we know how to have fun!!

STEVE KERZIE – "WILD HOSS"
The Chisholm paper highlighted the 1938 high school sports season and Kerz was a prominent figure.

"The individual stars of last year were Eino Oja, Steve Kerzie and Stan Kostka. Kerzie won regional honors in the broad jump and gathered fourth in the state meet in that event."

After graduating from Hibbing Junior College, Kerzie graduated from Morningside College in Sioux City, Iowa. He then joined the Air Force in June, 1942. After flying for 1-1/2 years and playing sports, he became athletic and recreation officer in the Phillipines, taught in Clinton, MN for one year and then came to Gilbert in 1949.

Kerz was teacher, coach, athletic director and referee. He retired from Gilbert in 1981.

At "Steve Kerzie Day on May 9, 1981", he was proclaimed the first referee to be presented with a cane and a seeing-eye dog by the Iron Range coaches.

Steve was a referee for 50 years in football and basketball and says he will retire this year after 60 years in track.

I met Steve when he became a volunteer at Ironworld. You couldn't find a more friendly and enthusiastic person. I think "fun" is Steve's middle name.

TALK FOR TWO
Poem written by Ernie Arola

Fair lady will you talk to me?
Situation now happens to be,
Gloomy, dreary and lonely too.
There is nothing like talk for two.
It might cheer things a little now,
Things might get better somehow.
When I go to bed tonight,
I can think that things are going right.
They are not really quite so bad,
As tonight was one of the best I had.

Ernie was quite a character. He played the fiddle and wrote poems and liked to entertain. This original was given to me by his son Mike Arola.

THE CHICKEN STORY THAT COULD ONLY HAPPEN TO A BLOND FROM SOUTH STURGEON

My friend Charlie and I were talking about old times. He said he raised chickens. I said, "How many chickens did you have?" What I heard was, "5,200 chickens". "What?", I said, "Where did you put them all?" He said, "Back there by the deer stands." I said, "Did you give any away?" "Of course", he replied, "maybe 7 or 8 chickens".

"Only 7 or 8 chickens, you have to be kidding".

What he was really saying, he had 50 to 100 chickens and I heard 5,200 chickens. We had a good laugh.

Also a quote from Jim Boubon (formerly of Side Lake)
when he and Paul Succio were up at Namikan 30 years ago.

"He who shall, so shall he who."
Jim, was your drink red with cherries in it?

A Minnesota State trooper pulled over a pickup on I-35.
The trooper asked, "Got any ID?"
The driver, a U of M graduate, replied, "Bout whut?"

WILLIAM SAINIO

This was written by Vienna Hobrle about her father William Sainio.

I am writing about my father. He was my idol, mentor and a family man. We were brought up with high ideals and an open mind. Even though both of my parents came from Finland, they settled in a mixed area with all kinds of people. We were taught not to be against any nationality or religion.....

When my dad went fishing, the family went along. My mother packed a bushel basket full of food. We went to Wynne Lake where Giants Ridge is now....That was about 75 years ago, I am 85 right now.

We were brought up with a strong faith and we belonged to the Independent Apostolic Lutheran Church. My dad was the cantor who started the singing. We did a lot of singing in our home.

The holidays were always fun as we celebrated them all. At Christmas my dad was Santa Claus. We did not know it until once I caught him, but pretended I did not see him. We were only allowed to get one thing and we thought about that all year long.

New Years was always special. We had to clean the house from top to bottom, take our baths, sauna, and put clean clothes on, so we would start New Years out right. We waited patiently for twelve o'clock midnight to come to hear the bells ring. My father opened the front door and the back door so the New Year chased the old year out of the back door. My father melted lead in a little pot and poured it into a pail of cold water. It would form a shape and you would put it against the wall to see what kind of a shadow it would make. This would tell your fortune. This custom was brought over from Finland and now I practice it myself. I have had the best of both worlds, depression and good times and am thankful for all the experiences. I guess you would call me a "pack sacker". I am not a Ranger or a Hibbingite by birth, even though I have been here 56 years.

Top L to R:
Clare Stanoff,
Judy Williams

Bottom L to R:
Tiny Tim, Mona,
Sister Carole Borovac

TINY TIM – The entertainer with the ukulele

While working at Ironworld in Chisholm, we booked a 50' and 60's group with about 6 or 7 entertainers and other popular groups of the time, The Cannibals, Herman from Herman's Hermits, Three Dog Nights and Tiny Tim. I forgot the names of the other groups. This was probably in 1987.

Co-worker Rob Gornick called to tell me they were staying overnight in Hibbing and since it was such a hot day, maybe they could come out to my lake home. I called my husband and told him it was going to be a very diverse group (under statement) and would it be all right. Yes, of course.

I told them we would furnish the food, but they had to buy their own beverages. Several of us went to Jack Frye's liquor store and they practically bought the store. I think he went on vacation right after that.

Tiny Tim was quite a character and the rest of the group was upset with him because he never changed his clothes or bathed. He wore the same red and white striped blazer from day to day.

We got the food together and called several people with jet boats and a few friends and away we went to Little Sturgeon.

Friend Vance was teaching many of them how to water ski. Most of them lived in Los Angeles and couldn't believe there was only several boats on the lake. Soon the word spread that there was something interesting happening at the Abel residence and boats started cruising very close to shore.

Vicki Gornick, well known organist and pianist was there and I dug out some of my WWI music and Tiny Tim and Miss Vicky performed.

Tiny Tim played the ukulele and sang "Oh Mona" to me. He also drank most of the owners Special Export.

The next day I received a lot of guff from people who were upset because they didn't get an invite. I told them I hardly knew about it.

The picture of the girls and Tiny Tim was used as my Christmas card one year. It read, "Merry Christmas to all and from Tiny Tim too." A friend called and said, "Who is that homely woman in that picture?" Life at Side Lake!

UNCLE LESTER WILLIAMS

My uncle was quite a guy. Gorgeous looking with curly, wavy dark hair. He played the drums in a band and would entertain everyone imitating Mario Lanza at any holiday gathering. There was nothing quiet about this man!

Our family moved to Iron Junction Road when I was 6 months old and after the war was over (WWII), Uncle Lester and family moved next to us. We shared the same driveway. Living 2-1/2 miles from Hibbing during this time was like living 100 miles from town.

Lester was always busy – you would find him in the basement sewing something for duck hunting or deer hunting season. Some days he was making pasties. He was a consummate inventor.

Uncle Lester followed in his dad's footprints and started working at the U.S. Steel mining division in 1935 as a laborer at the Hull Mine. His ambition was to be a locomotive engineer like his father. His biggest thrill was the day he served as fireman for his dad on one of the steamers. After coming back from the war, he discovered that the steam operated engines were on their way out and were being replaced by diesel equipment. He received a 25 year award for continuous service.

Uncle Lester is now in a Bigfork nursing home with Aunty Norma and how sad it is, they don't even know each other anymore.

JOHN BOROVAC, PHYSICAL FITNESS GURU

John was born in North Hibbing in 1913. When he was 12 years old, he got a job for a year with the Great Northern Railroad and made $.28 hour. He then decided to go back to school.

In the late 1920's and early 1930's there was no work, so John went "on the bum" – which literally meant, he jumped a train and wherever the train went, he would jump off and look for work. The Salvation Army and the area churches would feed these men. John worked for farmers taking in the grain.

In 1936 he began working for Pickands Mathers as a shovel operator and continued there until they closed in 1960.

In 1962 he went to Liberia, Africa with his wife Bernie, and worked as a shovel operator for two years. What a surprise, Bernie at age 46 and John, age 50, had a baby girl named Clare, their youngest of eight children.

They came back to Hibbing, but John went back to Africa for two more contracts. As he had a young child to support, he went to work at Pittsburgh Pacific at the age of 62 and worked until his late 60' when he finally retired for good.

John just turned 92 and still golfs, rides his bicycle 5 miles a day (sometimes 10) and is currently walking in the mall every day. Way to go, John!

MANX (ISLE OF MAN) AND CORNWALL

History about mining and my heritage....Manx (Isle of Man) and Cornwall.

It has often been said that a mine is a hole in the ground with a Cornishman at the bottom, and so true a saying, for Cornwall, being the very heart of mining world wide today, eventually brought many miners to the Isle of Man in the 1800's to seek and remove the riches from the ground. The earliest records show that man was extracting metal from the ground as long as 3000 years ago on many prehistoric site around the world using the simplest of tools such as the antlers from a deer to stone hammers.

Evidence of early workings on the Isle of Man can be seen on the northern cliffs....in the 13th century.

Evidence of bronze age activity was discovered near Laxey that suggests that the smelting and fusing of two metals may have occurred as early as 1700 BC. There are also places that produced haematite (their spelling).

In the mid 1800's, the Foxdale mine employed 250 men underground. An average of 3,500 tons of ore would be raised annually. The central mine worked until closure in 1911.

The Great Laxey, the most successful of mines, worked for over 150 years until its closure in 1929.

The mine had a total work force of more than 500 men in the 1850's and by the 1870's production reached its peak producing 2,500 ton of lead and silver, 9,000 tons of zinc and an average of 500 tons of copper annually.

Source: www.iomonline.co.im

YOU KNOW YOU ARE A REDNECK...if your grandmother has "Ammo" on her Christmas list.

Shriners /KC Bar- B-q
My dad forefront , Any Myrum, Ken Prothero,
John Brandt, Jim Juricich, Woody Frost, Angelo Taddie
7-21-78

**Joe Dimaggio at the
Dinah Shore Open
Palm Springs**

**Mona, Telly Savalas, and
Betty"Boop" Miller**

The Collyard Family-our Italian cousins.
We sure had fun times. Siiri was my Dad's sister.
Lewis, Siiri, Corky (in lap), Carlo, Johnny and Dewey.

Dad, Uncle Willy, & Ray
Hernesman, Lake Vermillion 1936

Aune Ruskanen wife of Wilho (Bill) Ruskanen in front of Suomi Ruskanen's farm house in Spudville. Taken around 1936.

John Dougherty

JOHN SUNDQUIST

The following was written by my brother-in-law, Dr. Ron Sundquist of White Bear Lake for his parent's 50th anniversary Memory Book. (Helen and John Sundquist)

"To Mom and Dad,

My earliest memory that has made an impact on my life, I carry with me to this day. It still occurs frequently when I am walking in the woods with my children. This memory happened when Russell and I were about 7-8 years old and went hunting with Dad, in the fall, up on the dumps. We were walking down a trail following Dad when he stopped and held up his hand for us to stop. A few seconds later a grouse walked across the trail and Dad shot it. At that time he stated, that if you pay close attention you will hear the movement and clucking of the grouse when they become nervous from having humans close by. We went on and hunted further for a number of hours, but the one thing that really impressed me was Dad's ability to understand what was going on in the woods. It didn't appear to me at that time, but through the years I have become more and more impressed with his knowledge and wisdom. This memory started out with nature and hunting and has expanded to all walks of life. When we understand our impact and presence in this world, we will have a better future."

Feb.24, 1912 – "N.E. Chapman, a Bear River farmer who raised the best potatoes in the U.S. was in Chisholm Saturday with a load of tubers which were sold for $1 a bushel."
<u>*Bear River Journal.*</u>

**Sister Patrice Jill with new husband
Ron Sundquist May 8th 1971**

GEORGE POGUE – SECOND MAYOR OF SOUTH STURGEON

I don't think anyone knows for sure how old George is nor do we care. He has given so many people so many laughs for so long - he is the original funster.

His older sister Audrey was my mother's maid of honor, so George has been around our family for a very long time.

His band played at my Jobs Daughters dance in 1957 (hate to give my age away) when I was a junior in high school.

When we bought our cabin in 1970 on South Sturgeon, he and his family had a cabin on the north side of the lake. His daughter now owns the place. There always was a commotion over there with a keg of beer on the beach and an interesting cast of characters. He had the same swimming trunks for years, though we thought they would rot away before the next season – no, they did not!

He had some heart troubles so would have to take nitro from time to time. One hot day friend Margy Retica and I took BobbyTerzich's paddleboat over to George's cabin. It was at the time that both of us wore two piece bathing suits (I never called them bikinis). Now Margy and I have always been called ample in a certain area and George saw us coming. He said all he could see were "breasts" (he used another word) and he had to take a nitro.

His trumpet was his life. He played in a band at the Highland Supper Club in Duluth and was also very active in the Shrine Circus and Ice Capades . He later played in the Mike Meier Band, The Gaslighters and the Talk-Abouts at various clubs around Duluth.

In his retirement years he still worked. I was leaving the Duluth airport one day and guess who was the security man at the gate – George!

There are so many George stories, I could fill a book. George, you are the greatest!

MY CORNISH GRANDFATHER – WILLIAM JACK WILLIAMS

Picture 1908 5th Ave. Hibbing

Grandpa was born in Ishpeming, Michigan in 1896. He grew up and met my grandmother Edith Cain in Ishpeming, married and had two children and then they moved to Northern Minnesota (Penobscot Location) in 1920. Penobscot was close to North Hibbing.

Grandpa worked at the Oliver Iron Mining Division's Sherman Mine as a locomotive engineer from 1921 and retired at the age of 65 in 1961. He worked 40 years at one place!

I remember Grandpa showing off when I was just a kid, walking on his hands throughout the entire house on 5th Avenue East.

Sister Carole and I would come in from the country and stay at their house on weekends. We thought this was great. We could walk to the State or Lybba Theatre and go to the Sweet Shop after the show.

Grandpa loved his retirement and the Twins. He would sit in his chair with his pipe or cigar in his mouth and the radio sat right next to him. He was totally at peace with the world.

He was a quiet and very patient kind man. He loved his gardens out at our country home.

Grandma and Grandpa didn't drink, but on holidays, the men would slip down into the basement and later come up laughing loudly. Grandpa always kept blackberry brandy on hand for medicinal purposes, of course.

He was also known for his homemade root beer. We are going to research this and hopefully come up the recipe.

Grandpa died on June 28, 1976 at the age of 80.

I still think of him fondly – here's to you Grandpa!

VINCE FORTI
SUNRISE BAKERY, HIBBING
ESTABLISHED 1913

Dad liked to cook; creating some kitchen competition. He was a great "doctor up the recipe" guy, and was partial to red pepper. My mother did not care for red pepper or dad in the kitchen. She was fortunate that he didn't retire until age 84.

Family, food and having a good time together was always the main event – and that we did!

Spaghetti was one of the few things my dad would eat, so I want to share his favorite sauce.

(See index for his spaghetti and meatball recipe.)

Submitted by his daughter, Barbara Forti Richards
For their catalog see: www.sunrisegourmet.com

ROBERT "BIBBS" MILLER

Bibbs grew up and attended school in Ft. Frances, Ontario, Canada. Anyone around here knows that the Canadian and Northern Minnesota boys were born with hockey sticks in their hands. Bibbs was one of them! His family had a hockey rink in the back yard and he played for the Orioles through high school.

A scout came to Fr. Frances, and in 1937 he was recruited by the Monarchs Hockey Team and came to Hibbing. The Monarchs were a pro team owned by Sandy McHardy and A. Panichi. The second and third season he played for the Monarchs and went to Hibbing Junior College. He then went to the University of Illinois for two years and also played hockey.

He joined the Navy and later was stationed in San Diego where he played under an assumed name so the Navy wouldn't know what he was doing.

He married beautiful Roberta Kerr from Hibbing when he was discharged from the Navy and they moved to Hibbing.

Bibbs is retired from his company B. Miller Products and resides in Side Lake, but we all know he would rather live part time in Palm Springs, California. His daughter Sally moved to Minnesota and now none of us knows where to go anymore in the winter.

"BIBBS" AND FRANK SINATRA

Did you know Bibbs has a very good singing voice? Yes, and he loves Frank.

On one of his trips to Palm Springs (I wasn't there unfortunately), he, Roberta and Sally and an assorted cast of characters, went out for dinner and at the nearby table sat Frank and Barbara Sinatra.

Barbara got up to go to the rest room and Bibbs said to Roberta, "Berta, go to the restroom with Barbara". Roberta wouldn't go and said to Bibbs, "what has she got that I haven't got". Bibbs waited patiently for Frank to go to the restroom, but it didn't happen. When I heard this story, I said, "Bibbs, you just wanted to come back to Side Lake and tell everyone you had it out with Frank Sinatra."

Too many Palm Springs stories to tell, so little time!

L to R: 1ST& 2ND unknown, 3RD ALFRED (PORKEY) PALUMBO,4TH unknown, PAUL LARSON, DICK THEIL, CHET FALK, BOB WILKEY and in the front NANCY WILKEY, child.

STORY ABOUT MY DAD
by Judy Larson.

Paul Larson was known for his steakfrying at the duck camp. He would stoke up the wood burning kitchen stove, throw on the iron skillets until they became red hot and throw on the steaks. He had been known to crack a few pans, but the smoke in the cabin and the heat made it impossible to see unless the doors were open.

An avid hunter, he was known for his accuracy and skill. He once saw a buck crossing the river and jumped on the hood of the car while Bill Rodgers drove to get to the spot before the deer,jumped off and shot his buck.

Also in the picture is Porkey Palumbo, who was known for his tuna spagetti for those Friday nights at the camp when all Fridays were meatless. His was a smokeless meal.

PAUL SERSHA

Paul Sersha, age 19, plays his father's Mervar button box at a family gathering at his home in West Eveleth in 1939.

After serving in the Civilian Conservation Corps and earning the reputation as the "fastest potato peeler" in camp, he later enlisted in the United States Coast Guard in World War II and served his country by guarding the homeland while stationed at the Statue of Liberty in New York City.

Paul and his wife Julie are 100% Slovenian and very proud of it. They both entertain (Julie plays the violin) at various venues around the area in their colorful and authentic Slovenian costumes.

WILHO (BILL) RUSKANEN

PHOTO: Wilho (Bill) Ruskanen's Gymnastic club in Cherry taken around 1928

Bill Ruskanen worked for the Oliver Iron Ore Mining Company. One week when he was working the night shift and was sleeping in the early afternoon, his mischievous wife, Aune, entered the bedroom and noticed his feet were not under the bed covers. She decided to paint his toenails with bright red nail polish. It wasn't until he visited the bathroom that he noticed that his toenails were red and he initially thought he was bleeding.

The following week, neighbor Joe asked Bill to go to the public sauna in Hibbing. Quiet, reserved Bill was mightily embarrassed when his toes were exposed to the other sauna "bull room" male guests.

Bill was born in Virginia in 1913 to parents who emigrated from Finland. He grew up in Cherry and moved to Spudville in 1937 when he married Aune Suomi. They had two children, Bette and Robert. Bill died in 1985.

(Our family would visit the Ruskanen and the Hernesman farms. We thought this was great fun, although I was a little afraid of the cows.)

Helpful Hints

To refinish antiques or revitalize wood, use equal parts of linseed oil, white vinegar, and turpentine. Rub into the furniture or wood with a soft cloth and lots of elbow grease.

To stop the ants in your pantry, seal off cracks where they are entering with putty or petroleum jelly. Also, try sprinkling .red pepper on floors and counter tops.

To fix sticking sliding doors, windows, and drawers, rub wax along their tracks.

To make a simple polish for copper bottom cookware, mix equal parts of flour and salt with vinegar to create a paste. Store the paste in the refrigerator.

Applying baking soda on a damp sponge will remove starch deposits from an iron. Make sure the iron is cold and unplugged.

Remove stale odors in the wash by adding baking soda.

To cleanTeflon™, combine 1 cup water, 2 tablespoons baking soda and ½ cup liquid bleach. Boil in stained pan for 5 to 10 minutes or until the stain disappears. Wash, rinse, dry, and condition with oil before using the pan again.

Corning Ware can be cleaned by filling it with water and dropping in two denture cleaning tablets. Let stand for 30 to 45 minutes.

A little instant coffee will work wonders on your wood furniture. Just make a thick paste from instant coffee and a little water, and rub it into the nicks and scratches on your dark wood furniture. You'll be amazed at how new and beautiful those pieces will look.

For a clogged shower head, boil it for 15 minutes in a mixture of ½ cup vinegar and 1 quart water.

For a spicy aroma, toss dried orange or lemon rinds into the fireplace. .

Add raw rice to the salt shaker to keep the salt free-flowing.

Ice cubes will help sharpen garbage disposal blades.

Separate stuck-together glasses by filling the inside one with cold water and setting them in hot water.

HIDDEN RECIPE
STAIRTS (Great for breakfast and the rest of the week!)
By Steve Mayer

Small Batch for me.
12 eggs,
Enough flour to thicken (Around 6 cups or more)
Then thin with milk 4 cups or more.
add water as needed to thin it more
Add Sugar, a cup at least.
Add ¼ cup oil to mixer

Mix together in the largest bowl you can find.

You want the batter to run easy into the skillet.

Heat large cast iron skillet (the biggest you can find) with ¼" or more of oil.

Pour batter into hot skillet and then use large spatula to stir up batter. The batter will clump but that's ok. You want to keep it cooking until the batter begins to form up into little balls about the size of a finger nail. Keep cutting up batter, until it all has formed into small chunks. Scoop onto plate and pour syrup over it.

 My Grandmother Gusty was taught this by her mother, and I love to make them. All the men in the family could eat a huge plate or bowl. For a smaller batch reduce the ingredients by ¾.

HERBS & SPICES

Acquaint yourself with herbs and spices. Add in small amounts, ¼ teaspoon for every 4 servings. Crush dried herbs or snip fresh ones before using. Use 3 times more fresh herbs if substituting fresh for dried.

Basil – Sweet warm flavor with an aromatic odor. Use whole or ground. Good with lamb, fish, roast, stews, ground beef, vegetables, dressing and omelets.

Bay Leaves – Pungent flavor. Use whol.e leaf but remove before serving. Good in vegetable dishes, seafood, stews and pickles.

Caraway – Spicy taste and aromatic smell. Use in cakes, breads, soups, cheese and sauerkraut.

Chives – Sweet, mild flavor like that of onion. Excellent in salads, fish, soups and potatoes.

Cilantro – Use fresh. Excellent in salads, fish, chicken, rice, beans and Mexican dishes.

Curry Powder – Spices are combined to proper proportions to give a distinct flavor to meat, poultry, fish and vegetables.

Dill – Both seeds and leaves are flavorful. Leaves may be used as a garnish or cooked with fish, soup, dressings, potatoes and beans. Leaves or the whole plant may be used to flavor pickles.

Fennel – Sweet, hot flavor. Both seeds and leaves are used. Use in small quantities in pies and baked goods. Leaves can be boiled with fish.

Ginger – A pungent root, this aromatic spice is sold fresh, dried or ground. Use in pickles, preserves, cakes, cookies, soups and meat dishes.

Marjoram – May be used both dried or green. Use to flavor fish, poultry, omelets, lamb, stew, stuffing and tomato juice.

Mint – Aromatic with a cool flavor. Excellent in beverages, fish, lamb, cheese, soup, peas, carrots, and fruit desserts.

HERBS & SPICES continued...

Oregano – Strong, aromatic odor. Use whole or ground in tomato juice, fish, eggs, pizza, omelets, chili, stew, gravy, poultry and vegetables.

Paprika – A bright red pepper, this spice is used in meat, vegetables and soups or as a garnish for potatoes, salads or eggs

Parsley – Best when used fresh, but can be used dried as a garnish or as a seasoning. Try in fish, omelets, soup, meat, stuffing and mixed greens.

Rosemary – Very aromatic. Can be used fresh or dried. Season fish, stuffing, beef, lamb, poultry, onions, eggs, bread and potatoes. Great in dressings.

Saffron – Orange-yellow in color, this spice flavors or colors foods. Use in soup, chicken, rice and breads.

Sage – Use fresh or dried, The flowers are sometimes used in salads. May be used in tomato juice, fish, omelets, beef, poultry, stuffing, cheese spreads and breads.

Tarragon – Leaves have a pungent, hot taste. Use to flavor sauces, salads, fish; poultry, tomatoes, eggs, green beans, carrots and dressings

Thyme – Sprinkle leaves on fish or poultry before broiling or baking. Throw a few sprigs directly on coals shortly before meat is finished grilling.

Measurements & Substitutions

Measurements

a pinch	1/8 teaspoon or less
3 teaspoons	1 tablespoon
4 tablespoons	1/4 cup
8 tablespoons	1/2 cup
12 tablespoons	3/4 cup
16 tablespoons	1 cup
2 cups	1 pint
4 cups	1 quart
4 quarts	1 gallon
8 quarts	1 peck
4 pecks	1 bushel
16 ounces	1 pound
32 ounces	1 quart
1 ounce liquid	2 tablespoons
8 ounces liquid	1 cup

**Use standard measuring spoons and cups.
All measurements are level.**

Substitutions

Ingredient	Quantity	Substitute
baking powder	1 teaspoon	¼ tsp. baking soda plus ½ tsp. cream of tartar
catsup or chili sauce	1 cup	1 c. tomato sauce plus ½ c. sugar and 2 T. vinegar (for use in cooking)
chocolate	1 square (1 oz.)	3 or 4 T. cocoa plus 1 T. butter
cornstarch	1. tablespoon	2 T. flour or 2 tsp. quick-cooking tapioca
cracker crumbs	¾ cup	1 c. bread crumbs
dates	1 lb.	1½ c. dates, pitted and cut
dry mustard	1 teaspoon	1 T. prepared mustard
flour, self-rising	1 cup	1 c. all-purpose flour, ½ tsp.salt, and 1 tsp. baking powder
herbs, fresh	1 tablespoon	1 tsp. dried herbs
milk, sour	1 cup	1 T. lemon juice or vinegar plus sweet
milk, whole	1 cup	½ c. evaporated milk plus ½ c. water (let stand 5 minutes)
min. marshmallows	10	1 lg. marshmallow
onion, fresh	1 small	1 T. instant minced onion, rehydrated
sugar, brown	1/2 cup	2 T. molasses in ½ c. granulated sugar
powdered	1 cup.	1 c. granulated sugar plus 1 tsp. cornstarch
tomato juice	1 cup	½ c. tomato sauce plus ½ c. water

**When substituting cocoa for chocolate in cakes, the amount of flour must be reduced.
Brown and white sugars usually can be interchanged.**

Food	Quantity	Yield
apple	1 medium	1 cup
banana, mashed	1 medium	1/3 cup
bread	1½ slices	1 cup soft crumbs
bread	1 slice	¼ cup fine, dry crumbs
butter	1 stick or ¼ pound	1/2 cup
cheese, American, cubed	1 pound	2-2/3 cups
American, grated	1 pound	5 cups
cream cheese	3-ounce package	6-2/3 tablespoons
chocolate, bitter	1 square	1 ounce
cocoa	1 pound	4 cups
coconut	1½ pound package	2-2/3 cups
coffee, ground	1 pound	5 cups
cornmeal	1 pound	3 cups
cornstarch	1 pound	3 cups
crackers, graham	14 squares	1 cup fine crumbs
saltine	28 crackers	1 cup fine crumbs
egg	4–5 whole	1 cup
whites	8-10	1 cup
yolks	10–12	1 cup
evaporated milk	1 cup	3 cups whipped
flour, cake, sifted	1 pound	4½ cups
rye	1 pound..	5 cups
white, sifted	1 pound	4 cups
white, unsifted	1 pound	3 ¾ cups
gelatin, flavored	3¼ ounces	½cup
unflavored	¼ ounce	1 tablespoon
lemon	1 medium	3 tablespoon juice
marshmallows	16	¼ pound
noodles, cooked	8-ounce package	7 cups
uncooked	4 ounces (1½ cups)	2–3 cups cooked
macaroni, cooked	8-ounce package	6 cups
macaroni, uncooked	4 ounces (1¼ cups)	2¼ cups cooked
spaghetti, uncooked	7 ounces	4 cups cooked
nuts, chopped	¼ pound	1 cup
almonds	1 pound	3 ½ cups
walnuts, broken	1 pound	3 cups
walnuts, unshelled	1 pound	1½–1¾ cups
onion	1 medium	½ cup
orange	3–4 medium	1 cup juice
raisins	1 pound	3½ cups
rice, brown	1 cup	4 cups cooked
converted	1 cup	3½ cups cooked
regular	1 cup	3 cups cooked
wild	1 cup	4 cups cooked
sugar, brown	1 pound	2 ½ cups
powdered	1 pound	3½ cups
white	1 pound	2 cups

Food Quantities

For Large Servings

	25 Servings	50 Serving	100 Servings
Beverages:			
coffee	½ pound and 1½ gallons water	1 pound and 3 gallons water	2 pounds and 6 gallons water
lemonade	10–15 lemons and 1½ gallons water	20–30 lemons and 3 gallons water	40–60 lemons and 6 gallons water
tea	1/12 pound and 1½ gallons water	1/6 pound and 3 gallons water	1/3 pound and 6 gallons water
Desserts:			
layered cake	1 - 12" cake	3 - 10" cakes	6 - 10" cakes
sheet cake	1 - 10" x 12" cake	1 - 12" x 20" cake	2 - 12" x 20" cakes
watermelon	37½ pounds	75 pounds	150 pounds
whipping cream	¾ pint	1½ to 2 pints	3–4 pints
Ice cream:			
brick	3¼ quarts	6½ quarts	13 quarts
bulk	2¼ quarts	4½ quarts or 1¼ gallons	9 quarts or 2½ gallons
Meat, poultry, or fish:			
fish	13 pounds	25 pounds	50 pounds
fish, fillets or steak	7½ pounds	15 pounds	30 pounds
hamburger	9 pounds	18 pounds	35 pounds
turkey or chicken	13 pounds	25–35 pounds	50–75 pounds
wieners (beet)	6½ pounds	13 pounds	25 pounds
Salads, casseroles:			
baked beans	¾ gallon	1¼ gallons	2½ gallons
jello salad	¾ gallon	1¼ gallons	2½ gallons
potato salad	4¼ quarts	2¼ gallons	4½ gallons
scalloped potatoes	4½ quarts or 1 - 12" x 20" pan	9 quarts or 2¼ gallons	18 quarts or 4½ gallons
spaghetti	1¼ gallons	2½ gallons	5 gallons
Sandwiches:			
bread	50 slices or 3 - 1 lb. loaves	100 slices or 6 - 1 lb. loaves	200 slices or 12 - 1 lb. loaves
butter	½ pound	1 pound	2 pounds
lettuce	1½ heads	3 heads	6 heads
mayonnaise	1 cup	2 cups	4 cups
mixed filling			
meat, eggs, fish	1½ quarts	3 quarts	6 quarts
jam, jelly	1 quart	2 quarts	4 quarts

Baking Desserts

Perfect Pies

1. Pie crust will be better and easier to make if all the ingredients are cool.
2. The lower crust should be placed in the pan so that it covers the surface smoothly. Air pockets beneath the surface will push the crust out of shape while baking.
3. Folding the top crust over the lower crust before crimping will keep juices in the pie.
4. In making custard pie, bake at a high temperature for about ten minutes to prevent a soggy crust. Then finish baking at a low temperature.
5. When making cream pie, sprinkle crust with powdered sugar in order to prevent it from becoming soggy.

Perfect Cakes

1. Fill cake pans two-thirds full and spread batter into corners and sides, leaving a slight hollow in the center.
2. Cake is done when it shrinks from the sides of the pan or if it springs back when touched lightly with the finger.
3. After removing a cake from the oven, place it on. a .rack for about five minutes. Then, the sides should be loosened and the cake turned out on a rack in order to finish cooling.
4. Do not frost cake, until thoroughly cool.
5. Icing will remain where you put it if you sprinkle cake with powdered sugar first.

Time and Temperature Chart

Dessert	Time	Temperature
butter cake, layer	20-40 min.	380° - 400°
butter cake, loaf	40-60 min.	360° - 400°
cake, angel	50-60 min.	300° - 360°
cake, fruit	3-4 hrs.	275° - 325°
cake, sponge	40-60 min.	300° - 350°
cookies, molasses	18-20 min.	350° - 375°
cookies, thin	10-12 min.	380° - 390°
cream puffs	45-60 min.	300° - 350°
meringue	40-60 min.	250° - 300°
pie crust	20-40 min.	400° - 500°

HIBBING **Park** HOTEL & SUITES

120 Guest Rooms * Exercise Room

Pool * Sauna * Hot Tub

Meetings & Convention Services

Grandma's IN THE Park
Bar & Grill
HIBBING, MINNESOTA

1402 East Howard Street

Hibbing, MN 55746

(218)262-3481

1 (800) 262-3481

fax (218) 262-1906

www.hibbingparkhotel.com

E-mail: hibbpark@rangebroadband.com

Get additional copies of this cookbook by returning an order form and your check or money order to:

Mona J. Abel
13039 Memory Lane
Side Lake, MN 55781

Please send me_____copies of **To Dad With Love** for **$18.00** per copy plus **$2.95** for shipping& handling per book.and $1.17 MN sales tax per book.
Enclosed is my check or money order for $_____

Mail Books To:

Name _____

Address _____

City_____

State - Zip _____

_____
Signed

Or order online by credit card at:

http://www.cookbooksbymona.com

NOTES

NOTES